Latimer Briefing 20

CW00537371

Transgender Liturgies

Should the Church of England develop liturgical materials to mark gender transition?

by Martin Davie

The Latimer Trust

CONTENTS

Introduction

In April 2015 Blackburn Diocesan Synod passed the following motion:

That this Synod, recognising the need for transgender people to be welcomed and affirmed in their parish church, calls on the House of Bishops to consider whether some nationally commended liturgical materials might be prepared to mark a person's gender transition.

The purpose of this study is to consider whether it would be right for the members of General Synod to vote in favour of this motion.

The study is in five chapters.

Chapter 1 explains in more detail what the motion proposes and the theological implications of passing it.

Chapter 2 looks at how the case for the acceptance of gender transition is made out in three representative documents, Christina Beardsley's paper 'The transsexual person is my neighbour,' Chris Dowd's chapter 'Five things cis folk don't know about trans folk because it isn't on trashy TV – my right of reply' and Justin Tanis' book *Transgendered – Theology, Ministry and Communities of Faith.*

Chapter 3 presents a critical analysis of what is said in these documents, explaining why it does not provide a convincing basis for accepting the idea at the heart of gender transition that someone's true self can be separated from their biological sex.

Chapter 4 sets out an alternative Christian theological framework for approaching the issue of gender transition and for giving pastoral care for transgender people.

Chapter 5 explains why what is said in the previous chapters means that it would not be right to support the Blackburn motion.

The three appendices at the end of the report contain additional resources from the Lutheran Church – Missouri Synod and the Southern Baptist Convention which relate to how we should view the transgender issue from a Christian theological perspective and how we should offer pastoral care to transgender people.

In line with the wording of the Blackburn report the term 'transgender people' will generally be used in this report. However, the synonymous terms 'transsexual people' and 'trans folk' will also be used in quotations from, or references to, other documents.

1. What does the Blackburn motion propose?

The starting point for the Blackburn motion is the belief that 'transgender people' need to be 'welcomed and affirmed' in their parish churches.

As the briefing paper by Christina Beardsley in support of the motion explains: 'The transgender people referred to in the motion are those who have made, or are in the process of making, a permanent gender transition.' As the paper further explains 'Transition is the process by which one adopts the gender expression that matches one's gender identity.'[1]

The term 'gender identity' means a person's internal sense of their sexual identity, their personal understanding of who they truly are. There are some people who would say that they have a 'non-binary' sense of their sexual identity since they would not identify themselves as being either male or female.[2] However the vast majority of human beings see themselves as being either male or female and for the vast majority of these people their sense of being either male or female is in accordance with their biology. They have male biology and feel that they are male, or they have female biology and feel that they are female (the current technical term for this is 'cisgender'). However, there are some people who are 'transgender' since they suffer from what is known as 'gender dysphoria' in that they have male biology but feel that they are really a woman or have female biology but feel that they are really a man.[3]

Those who undergo a process of gender transition seek to live in accordance with what they feel is their true gender identity rather than according to their biology. Thus in a male to female transition someone who is biologically male will live as a woman, adopt a female name and may undergo hormone treatment and surgery to seek to make their body more female in appearance. Conversely, in female to male transition someone who is biologically female will live as a man, adopt a male name and may undergo hormone treatment and surgery to seek to make their body more male in appearance.

---

[1] Christina Beardsley, 'Welcoming transgender people and responding to their needs' at http://changingattitude.org.uk/archives/8542.

[2] See http://www.nonbinary.org/wiki/Nonbinary_gender

[3] One estimate is that 0.2% of the population may feel this way, but this figure is disputed.

Under the Gender Recognition Act of 2004 someone who has undergone transition may apply for a 'gender recognition certificate' after having lived for two years in their 'acquired gender' and when a full certificate is issued 'the person's gender becomes for all purposes the acquired gender (so that, if the acquired gender is the male gender, the person's sex becomes that of a man and, if it is the female gender, the person's sex becomes that of a woman).'[4] To put it simply, once a full gender recognition certificate has been granted someone who was once legally a man becomes legally a woman and vice versa.

As we have already noted, the position taken by the Blackburn motion is that those who have gone through transition, or who are in the process of doing so, need to be both 'welcomed' and 'affirmed' by their parish churches. The significance of the word 'affirmed' is that the people concerned should not simply be welcomed (which might go alongside non-acceptance of, or ambivalence about, their gender transition), but should be affirmed either in the transition they have made or the one that they are making. In the case of male to female transition, for example, it would mean those in their parish church affirming either that they have become a woman, or that they are in the process of becoming a woman.

On the basis of this perceived need for affirmation, what the motion asks the House of Bishops to do in the context of their role of overseeing the development of the Church of England's liturgy is to consider the possibility of developing services 'to mark a person's gender transition' that the House could then commend for use across the Church of England on a permissive basis.

What is meant by 'marking a person's gender transition' is using liturgy to affirm before God that transition has taken place, so that someone who was regarded as male is now recognised as female or vice versa and to bless and/or pray for them in their new identity. We can see this in the two examples of such liturgies provided by Christina Beardsley in her article 'A service of affirmation and blessing for a Trans person'.[5]

---

4   Gender Recognition Act 2004, 9(1) at *Gender Recognition Act 2004*
    http://www.legislation.gov.uk/ukpga/2004/7/crossheading/consequences-of-issue-
    of-gender-recognition-certificate-etc
5   Christina Beardsley , 'A service of affirmation and blessing for a Trans person' at A
    service of affirmation and blessing for a Trans person : Changing Attitude
    http://changingattitude.org.uk/archives/7294

The first example is a rite developed in the United States by the Lutheran Pastor Nadia Bolz-Weber on the basis of material from an Episcopal Priest, Michele Morgan.

This rite was used to mark the female to male transition of someone previously called Mary to someone called Asher. It runs as follows (Lindsey and Kate are members of the congregation and Pr.Nadia is Pastor Nadia Bolz-Weber):

Presider: Holy One of Blessing, in baptism you bring us to new life in Jesus Christ and you name us Beloved. We give you thanks for the renewal of that life and love in Mary Christine Callahan, who now takes on a new name.

Strengthen and uphold him as he grows in power, and authority, and meaning of this name: we pray in the Name above names, Jesus, your Son, whom with you and the Holy Spirit, the Triune God, we adore. Amen

(Lindsey) A reading from the letter of Paul to the Galatians:

There is no longer Jew or Greek, there is no longer slave or free, there is no longer male and female; for all are one in Christ Jesus.

The word of the Lord

Thanks be to God

(Laying on of hands)

Let us pray:

We pray for your servant Asher, with thanks for the journey and awakening that have brought him to this moment, for his place amongst your people, and for his gifts and calling to serve you.

O God, in renaming your servants Abraham, Sarah, Jacob, Peter, and Paul, you gave them new lives and new tasks, new love and new hope.

We now hold before you our companion. Bless him with a new measure of grace as he takes this new name. Write him again in your heart and on your palm.

And grant that we all be worthy to call ourselves Christians, for the sake of your Christ whose name is Love, and in whom, with you and the Spirit, we pray. Amen

The Giving of the name

Pr. Nadia: By what name shall you be known?

Kate: The name shall be Asher

Asher: My name is Asher

The community may respond by repeating

Your name shall be Asher

Pr. Nadia: Bear this name in the Name of Christ. Share it in the name of Mercy. Offer it in the name of Justice.

Christ is among us making peace right here right now. The peace of Christ be with you all. And also with you.[6]

The second example is an unofficial service from the Church of England. It is called 'Emerging into the light' and it is a service of 'affirmation and blessing' created by the Revd. Julie Robson, the curate of St. Andrew's Church, Corbridge, to mark the male to female transition of Susan Musgrove.[7]

The service, which was held on 20th April 2013, runs as follows:

Welcome.
Rev David Hewlett
Vicar of Corbridge

Introduction.
We stand to sing:
Hymn no 723 The Lord is my Shepherd (Psalm 23)

Reading.
Galatians 3:23-28
read by: Jenny Black

The choir sing: *Pie Jesu*

Address.
Rev Cecilia Eggleston
Pastor of the Metropolitan Community Church,
Newcastle Upon Tyne

---

6   Text at http://www.patheos.com/blogs/nadiabolzweber/2012/01/liturgical-naming-rite-for-a-transgendered-church-member/
7   The name Susan is used here because that was the name used at the service. It does not imply any judgement on the actual sex of the person concerned.

The Mirror Lied.
read by: Peter Dorrant

Hymn.
> I will change your name
> You shall no longer be called
> Wounded, outcast, lonely or afraid.
> I will change your name
> Your new name shall be
> Confidence, joyfulness
> Overcoming one, faithfulness,
> Friend of God, One who seeks my face.

We kneel or sit to pray

The Prayers.

The Lord's Prayer

Anointing and affirmation of Baptism Vows.

Praise God who made heaven and earth

All. who keeps his promise for ever

Let us give thanks to the Lord our God

All. who is worthy of all thanksgiving and praise

Blessed are you sovereign God, gentle and merciful.

Your Word brought light out of darkness and daily your Spirit renews creation.

You Son brought healing, love and freedom so inspiring us to praise your name for ever.

By the power of your Spirit may your blessing rest upon Susan whom we anoint with this Oil of Chrism in your name.

May she be whole in body, mind and spirit; and live a life of service as a cherished daughter in your kingdom.

Through Christ our Lord we lift our voices in thanks and praise

All. Blessed be God, our strength and our salvation now and for ever. Amen.

[the congregation joins Susan in affirming our baptism vows]

In baptism, God calls us out of darkness into his marvellous light. To follow Christ means dying to sin and rising to new life with him.

Therefore I ask: Do you turn to Christ?

They reply : **I turn to Christ.**

Do you repent of your sins?

They reply: **I repent of my sins.**

Do you renounce evil?

They reply: **I renounce evil.**

Then Choir sing : *Jubilate*

The Blessing.

We stand to sing: Hymn no 152 Dear Lord and Father of Mankind.[8]

These two services are different in form, but what they have in common is that they both involve an affirmation before God that the identity that someone has legally acquired as a result of a process of gender transition is their true identity. That is to say, they affirm that Asher really is male (hence the use of 'him') and that Susan really is female (hence the use of 'she' and 'daughter').

The theological question these services raise is whether it is possible to make such an affirmation.

Asher was born with a female body and Susan was born with a male one and both these bodies still exist even after their transition (even hormone treatment and sexual reconstruction surgery cannot abolish the basic biological sex of a body). The issue that has to be addressed is therefore whether from a theological perspective someone who has a female body can truly be a man and whether someone who has a male body can be truly a woman. Is it possible to have a true gender identity that is contrary to one's biology?

The Church of England's current official stance on this matter is set out in the House of Bishops Memo HB(03)M1 which records the view taken by the House of Bishops in 2003. This states:

The House recognised that there was a range of views within the Church on transsexualism and accepted that (as matters stood at present) both the positions set out below could properly be held:

a) some Christians concluded on the basis of Scripture and Christian anthropology, that concepts such as 'gender

---

[8] Text at http://changingattitude.org.uk/wp-content/uploads/2013/07/Order-of-Service-1.pdf

reassignment' or 'sex change' were really a fiction. Hormone treatment or surgery might change physical appearance, but they could not change the fundamental God-given reality of 'male and female He created them'.

b) others, by contrast, whilst recognising that medical opinion was not unanimous, were persuaded that there were individuals whose conviction that they were 'trapped in the wrong body' was so profound and persistent that medical intervention, which might include psychiatric, hormone, and surgical elements, was legitimate and that the result could properly be termed a change of sex or gender.

The House agreed that the Church should continue to engage in discussions with the Lord Chancellor's Department with a view to safeguarding the position of bishops unwilling to ordain transgendered candidates and, once marriage of transsexuals became possible in law, securing an exemption for clergy not willing to solemnise such marriages.9

The last paragraph refers to the discussions that were taking place with the Government prior to the introduction of the *Gender Recognition Act* in 2004.

The line taken by this memo means that the Church of England currently does not have an agreed position on the question of whether someone can be truthfully said to have a male or female identity that is at variance with their biological sex. However, if the House of Bishops were to commend services to mark gender transition along the lines of the services quoted in this chapter this would mean that the Church of England would have decided *de facto* that it would be right to affirm that this is the case.

In line with a tradition going back to the early centuries of the Church, the Church of England holds that liturgy expresses what the Church believes (as the Latin tag puts it, *lex orandi, lex credendi*) and therefore commending the sort of services we have looked at in this chapter would involve saying that the Church of England believes that someone who is biologically male can in fact be female and vice versa.

It might be argued in response that if the services concerned were ones that could be used, but did not have to be, this would mean that that the Church of England was recognising that some people within it

---

9   Text in http://changingattitude.org.uk/archives/8542

believe that it is possible to be a woman with male biology and vice versa, without committing the Church of England as a whole to this position. However, if we accept that the House of Bishops, acting on behalf of the Church of England, does not commend liturgical statements which it believes to be untrue, it follows that the commendation of such services would mean that the Church of England as a whole accepts the truth of the claim implied in them that someone can be a woman with male biology and vice versa. Some people might still dissent from it, but this would be the Church of England's position.

In the remainder of this report we shall consider the question of whether this would be a good position for the Church of England to adopt. In the next chapter we shall begin this consideration by looking at the case for the adoption of this position made out in three representative documents.

2. The case for accepting gender transition.

In this chapter we shall look at the case for the acceptance of gender transition set out in three documents which have been chosen because what they say is representative of the arguments that are generally put forward in support of such acceptance.

2.1. *Christina Beardsley 'The Transsexual person is my neighbour.'*

Christina Beardsley's 2007 paper 'The Transsexual person is my neighbour' is a set of guidelines written 'to assist Christian leaders who are approached by a transsexual person, or their family, for pastoral support.'[1]

In her paper Beardsley explains that 'Many transsexual people have travelled a difficult road, and the process of transition may have cost them their marriage or partner, children, or job' and that 'These are the sort of issues they might wish to discuss with their pastor.'

Her advice to those who have pastoral encounters with transsexual people is:

> Try not to be shocked if the short young man or the tall blonde woman in front of you explains that their birth sex was different from their currently perceived gender. Attend to them, as you would to any other child of God for whom Christ died. Do not judge. This person is likely to have experienced much pain and hurt already. Or, again, it may be that they are very aware of the incompleteness of their transition. Whatever the circumstances, the last thing they need is to be condemned and rejected. By the grace of God, and with the help of contemporary medical care, this person has at last found some peace of mind and a sounder basis for discovering their true self. Be there for them now in the name of the Lord and help them on their journey of faith.[2]

---

[1] Christina Beardsley, 'The Transsexual person is my neighbour' p 1, text at http://changingattitude.org.uk/resources/publications/the-transsexual-person-is-my-neighbour.

[2] Beardsley, 'The Transsexual person is my neighbour', p 4.

She goes on to say that if the person who comes forward for pastoral support is someone who has not yet gone through transition then:

> ...they are likely to be suffering intensely. Many transsexual people realise their condition early in life but have tried to conform to gender stereotypes under pressure from their family and society, combined with the fear of rejection. Some have endured abuse and bullying as children, while others may have been subjected to aversion therapy, so wounds will go deep. Their condition may have been a closely guarded secret, and a source of guilt, due to their inability to be rid of a desire that is sometimes seen as a lifestyle choice rather than a natural human variation.

> Trans women, in particular, are likely to have made great efforts to be 'normal' including marriage and raising children, and some go to enormous lengths to prove to themselves and others that their gender identity matches their perceived gender; e.g. participating in macho sports activities or joining the armed services. When the painful truth becomes clear that they have been 'living a lie' the individual concerned can often sink into deep depression, which may lead to alcohol and drug abuse. The old feelings of guilt are now compounded by the thought that they have failed to conquer their condition and that this could have serious consequences for their spouse and family. There is also the fear of attempting to make a new start in life. At this stage some may commit suicide. The fear of rejection learnt in childhood often prevents people from seeking help so that suicide may seem the only way out.

> Some trans men experience another kind of distress due to the mismatch between their perceived gender and their identity. Even before transition they may be regarded, visually at least, as males, and can enhance this by adopting a short haircut, a unisex name and clothing. However, once they start to speak people's perception often changes and they are assumed to be female instead and addressed accordingly as 'madam' rather than 'sir'. This discrepancy between appearance and perception, which is acutely painful for the trans man concerned (since people appear to be thwarting his attempts to be himself) is also experienced by trans women, especially in the early days of transition or if they fail to feminise appropriately.[3]

Beardsley emphasises that:

---

[3]   Beardsley, 'The Transsexual person is my neighbour', pp 4-5.

....if a transsexual person seeks your help at any of these stages they will be one of the most vulnerable people you are likely to meet. Being judgemental and implying that God does not approve of them may be the final straw that pushes them over the edge. Remember too that this is a specialist area and be ready to refer to others, including the Samaritans.[4]

Having given this pastoral advice, Beardsley turns to the medical and scientific aspects of transsexualism. She writes that over the past fifty years:

...medicine and science have come to recognise the validity of transsexual people's experience and the appropriateness of hormonal and surgical intervention. Prior to that the medical solution was to treat the person as insane and prescribe aversion therapy, which was usually ineffective. Research in this area is still in its infancy but the authors of *Transsexualism: The Current Medical Viewpoint* (1996) concluded that 'the weight of current scientific evidence suggests a biologically-based, multi-factorial aetiology for transsexualism'. The finding of a Dutch research team which showed 'a female brain structure in genetically male transsexuals and supports the hypothesis that gender identity develops as a result of an interaction between the developing brain and sex hormones,' has helped to underpin the prevailing medical treatment.[5]

She also stresses that transsexualism is not a form of mental illness.

Although Gender Identity Disorder is included in the latest (American) *Diagnostic and Statistical Manual of Mental Disorders* (IV) it is not strictly a mental health problem, even though hormone therapy and surgery normally require two psychiatric referrals. Here the psychiatrist's role is to ensure that the person is not exhibiting signs of mental illness and is sufficiently psychologically robust to endure the rigours of transition. In a pastoral encounter it would be wise to check that the person has been referred to, or is already under, the care of a consultant psychiatrist, especially as gender confusion can sometimes mask an underlying mental health condition, e.g. schizophrenia.[6]

Beardsley next moves on to consider 'Christian perspectives' on transsexualism. She starts by looking at the Bible and begins her

---

4   Beardsley, 'The Transsexual person is my neighbour', p 5.
5   Beardsley, 'The Transsexual person is my neighbour', p 6.
6   Beardsley, 'The Transsexual person is my neighbour', p 6.

examination of its teaching by declaring that the Bible does not directly address the issue of 'cross-gender identification and behaviour' even though 'a few verses are sometimes quoted as if it did.'[7] Among the verses Beardsley has in mind are Deuteronomy 22:5 and Genesis 1:27 and she considers each of these verses in turn.

On Deuteronomy 22:5 she writes:

Dressing in the clothes of the opposite gender is forbidden in Deuteronomy 22:5, which is part of a series of regulations that also prohibit the mixing, or blending, of various foods and fibres. Although Jesus challenged this religious obsession with purity, and early Christianity included Gentile (non-Jewish) Christians, who did not observe many of the Old Testament laws, some people would argue that this prescription against cross-dressing still obtains. However, it is important to remember that, prior to transition, the transsexual person is not the gender that they are perceived to be. They are a genetic female with male gender identity or a genetic male with female gender identity. It is distressing for such people to assume the clothes and social behaviour of their birth sex – that, for them, feels like 'cross-dressing' – and totally appropriate for them to dress and behave in ways which express their true gender identity.

In any case, a brief review of the history of Western clothing shows that fashion has often blurred these boundaries: trousers, for example, once a staple of the male wardrobe, are worn by the majority of women today, while the development of unisex styles, especially for the young, has become standard.[8]

On Genesis 1:27 she notes that the words 'male and female He created them' are often quoted: 'to support the view that the Creator, or nature, offer human beings only two options, man or woman, and that one's birth sex is a 'given' that one should not seek to alter.'[9] However, she writes:

What this verse actually says – 'God created man in his own image; in the image of God he created him; male and female He created them' – broadens its meaning considerably, placing the emphasis, not so much on the policing of gender boundaries, but on the dignity of human beings, men and women, made in the image of God.[10]

---

7   Beardsley, 'The Transsexual person is my neighbour', p 6.
8   Beardsley, 'The Transsexual person is my neighbour', pp 6-7.
9   Beardsley, 'The Transsexual person is my neighbour', p 7.
10   Beardsley, 'The Transsexual person is my neighbour', p 7.

Moreover, Beardsley adds:

> '...the argument from nature in favour of just two sexes is seriously challenged by the genetic and physical variations that actually occur, as a conversation with maternity unit staff will confirm.'[11]

Beardsley goes on to say that these two verses from the Old Testament are 'often quoted as if the Bible were a rule-book to regulate human behaviour' whereas modern theologians:

> ....have tended to approach the Bible as a record of the broad sweep of salvation history, rather than a set of detailed regulations: God's evolving relationship with human beings through Jesus Christ, which is characterised by grace rather than law.[12]

She also explains how this new approach has led transsexual people to find fresh spiritual resources within the biblical text.

> Inspired by this wider framework, transsexual people – especially trans women – have explored the biblical texts about God's graceful inclusion of eunuchs, under both the Old and New Covenant (Isaiah 56:4,5; Acts 8:26-40; and perhaps Matthew 19:12). Here they have tapped into a rich strand of biblical tradition, in which God shows special tenderness and pity to the childless and barren, that is largely obscured by the contemporary Church's focus on marriage and procreation.

> St Paul's declaration in Galatians 3:28 that 'in Christ there is ... neither male nor female' is a text that energised and encouraged those who argued for the ordination of women as priests in the Church of England. This belief that gender distinctions, and the power distortions that they attract, are overcome by Christ, is a profoundly moving one; taken together with Genesis 1:27 it suggests that God in Christ transcends gender, and that Christians should seek to avoid the 'fallen' aspects of gender difference.

> This transformative effect of Christ's work for the whole of creation, powerfully expressed in Romans 8, offers a deeply Christian vision and context for interpreting the Bible, and one in which transsexual people can begin to make sense of their experiences. The images of journeying in faith, adopting a new name, embracing death and resurrection, or becoming a new creation, which are deeply embedded in the Bible and of universal application, can assume a

---

11   Beardsley, 'The Transsexual person is my neighbour', p 7.
12   Beardsley, 'The Transsexual person is my neighbour', p 7.

special nuance for transsexual people as they undergo gender re-assignment.[13]

Having considered the Bible, Beardsley then moves on to explain the position on transsexualism taken by the Roman Catholic Church, the Evangelical Alliance, the Church of England and the Metropolitan Community Church. She is critical of the opposition to gender transition by both the Roman Catholic Church and the Evangelical Alliance.

On the position taken by the Roman Catholic Church she writes:

Roman Catholic objections to medical intervention and surgery for transsexual people tend to be based on the 'natural law' tradition that has played such a significant role in Catholic theology. Despite scientific evidence of gender variation in nature, including human beings, gender re-assignment is said to subvert the 'natural' order of male and female, and a Church that is so strongly opposed to artificial birth control is hardly likely to condone the self-castration or loss of fertility it entails.[14]

On the position taken by the Evangelical Alliance she states:

The Evangelical Alliance report *Transsexuality* also approaches the subject from dogmatic presuppositions rather than a pastoral standpoint. According to this document, the self-evident nature of male and female gender, immutably fixed by human physiology, and supported by the Scriptures, renders the very notion of 'changing gender' to be impossible. This tendency to define gender (and sexuality) in disproportionately biological terms, which it shares with Roman Catholicism, is somewhat surprising given Jesus' belief that 'the kingdom of God is within you.'[15]

She further notes that the authors of the Evangelical Alliance's report:

....are very uncomfortable with the idea of the body being adjusted to the mind; instead they advocate that the mind must be adjusted to the body. This belief in the possibility of a psychological resolution of transsexualism may be due to the emphasis on inward conversion in Evangelicalism. However, it fails to acknowledge the repeated failure of psychological 'cures', let alone the actual experience of transsexual people, particularly the lengths that some will go to

---

13 Beardsley, 'The Transsexual person is my neighbour', p 7.
14 Beardsley, 'The Transsexual person is my neighbour', p 8.
15 Beardsley, 'The Transsexual person is my neighbour', p 8.

conform to their birth sex before they finally admit their condition. It also ignores the fact that the treatment of Gender Dysphoria by hormone therapy and surgery has become a standard and successful procedure within the NHS and private practice after nearly eighty years' experience of surgery.[16]

After looking at Church teaching and noting the existence of the Sibyls, the Christian transgender support group, Beardsley then returns to the issue of how Christian communities should respond to transsexual people. She writes that while 'respect and love for the transsexual person should be the norm' in practice:

> ... communities – even Christian ones – can exert all sorts of pressures, subtle or otherwise, conscious or unconscious, to 'persuade' people who are different to conform to group expectations.

> Sadly this has been the experience of many Christian transsexual people. Some have been threatened with excommunication, or told that they will never be able to assume a church office or responsibility if they continue with transition. Some trans people have felt humiliated and excluded when a church has banned them from using the toilet appropriate to their transition, or from any toilet on church premises, or insisted that they use the disabled toilet (because of its unisex status). This is pure prejudice as no one is at any harm or risk from the transsexual person. Moreover, if transition is to be real the person must be allowed to use the toilets appropriate to their gender identity and changing perceived gender. On the other hand, some pastors and congregations have lovingly accepted a Christian transsexual or a transgendered individual, dealing sensitively with practical issues such as the use of toilets, and the hope is that this would happen in the majority of cases.[17]

Beardsley notes that the greatest difficulties can occur when someone begins the process of transition.

> The reaction may be shock and disbelief. This person may be a spouse and/or a parent, and everyone has assumed that they are the man or the woman that they appear to be; now they are saying the very opposite. Gender is not black and white, however: each of us is a mixture of masculine and feminine, some people being more strongly one than the other, and when someone declares that they might be a different gender identity from the one they are perceived

---

16   Beardsley, 'The Transsexual person is my neighbour', p 8.
17   Beardsley, 'The Transsexual person is my neighbour', p 12.

to be it can cause uncertainty for some of the people around them. Usually this is a brief phase. People may be forced to look at themselves and they might have their own confusions to deal with. It is important that personal gut reactions do not become wrapped up with biblical texts and dogmatic pronouncements, as the combination of emotional response and apparently authoritative teaching can be a harmful and destructive one.[18]

She also notes that when someone discloses their intention to undertake transition it may then be necessary for those supporting them to draw on the assistance of those with specialist experience.

A person disclosing their intention to proceed with gender re-assignment will have reached a critical point in their lives and they and their family will be looking for support and understanding from their church community. As Gender Dysphoria is a specialist matter affecting a minority of people there can be no expectation that the local church should have any expertise in this area. Continuing to be treated like any other member of the congregation ought to be the norm, and the support needed may be simply that of loving friendship and a regular listening ear. In one church someone was identified to befriend the trans person and simply listen to them on a monthly basis. Advice on how to find a spiritual director, usually a specialist beyond the local congregation, might also be helpful. These options could be made available to partners as well. The support of partners and their children is an important but specialised area, and it is advisable to direct people to an appropriate organisation, such as Depend.

By this point the person concerned is likely to know of specialist sources of help and the congregation could draw on these. The Gender Trust can provide information, advice and speakers. It would be wise to invite someone from the Gender Trust if the person's decision to transition is to be formally communicated to the congregation. In the workplace the communication to other employees or staff will have been handled very professionally and no less should be expected in the church setting, though in the majority of cases such formality will be unnecessary, as other members of the congregation will gradually hear of what is happening, begin to observe the changes, and continue to accept the person as they always have.[19]

---

18 Beardsley, 'The Transsexual person is my neighbour', pp 12-13.
19 Beardsley, 'The Transsexual person is my neighbour', p 13.

In a further section of her paper looking at number of ethical issues relating to transsexualism, Beardsley addresses the issue of self-fulfilment versus self-sacrifice in relation to people who undergo gender transition and argues that the choice between the two is less straightforward than it is often presented as being.

> Transsexual people who transition are sometimes accused of selfishness for putting their personal needs above other considerations and, if they are Christians, reminded of the virtue of self-denial. Here the choice is presented as if it were a simple one between the worldly ideal of self-fulfilment and the religious ideal of self-sacrifice, but moral choices are rarely that straightforward. Transition can involve considerable sacrifice for those who proceed with it, and while they may eventually flourish psychologically and spiritually there will have been many losses on the way. In any case, Christian ethics regards love as far more significant than renunciation – though love may require precisely that – and in Jesus' teaching love of self is seen as key to loving others. When someone transitions their self-esteem often increases because they have begun to love themselves as they truly are, instead of pretending to be someone else. One also has to bear in mind the psychological and social cost in terms of depression etc. of maintaining that pretence, though people often do, usually so as not to hurt their partner or family. Only when internal defences begin to break down and the façade starts to crumble do relatives appreciate the distress their loved one has been living with and the love and sacrifice that will be required of them as well, whatever the outcome may be.[20]

Beardsley concludes her paper by commenting that there are:

> ....many people who live with a deep confusion about their gender identity, the majority of whom are probably not transsexual, but who nevertheless need a great deal of help and support to understand themselves better.[21]

As she sees it:

> Whenever someone presents with a problem of gender identity the best form of help a Christian community can provide is a loving and accepting environment in which the person can gain the confidence to find out whether or not they are transsexual. Once their diagnosis

---

[20] Beardsley, 'The Transsexual person is my neighbour', pp 14-15.
[21] Beardsley, 'The Transsexual person is my neighbour', p 16.

has been confirmed they may or may not wish to transition, and, if they prove not to be transsexual, they face the question, 'what now?' In each of these circumstances, pastors and congregations can play an important role in helping people explore the complex reality of what it means to be a human being made in the Divine image.[22]

2.2. Chris Dowd : Five things cis folk don't know about trans folk

Chris Dowd's chapter 'Five things cis folk don't know about trans folk because it isn't on trashy TV – my right of reply' is his response to the assumptions about transgender people that he came across while undertaking research for his 2014 Birmingham University doctoral thesis 'Transfaith: An exploration of gender in the Church from the margins.'

The first of these assumptions is that there is a simple binary division between men and women. To attempt to make sense of transgender people within this framework gender transition is understood in medical terms as a process in which by means of the appropriate medical treatment someone moves from being a man to being a woman and vice versa.

> On many occasions I have heard gender dysphoria described as a birth defect where 'people are born in the wrong body. After treatment the trans person is cured and they are safely on the other side of the gender binary (reaffirming that there is only male and female) and there is a happy ending to an awkward story.[23]

According to Dowd, this view of the matter 'obscures more reality than it admits.' This is because what he learned in the course of his research is that 'transitioning isn't primarily a medical procedure but a psychological and spiritual one.'[24] For those trans folk he interviewed for his research, he writes:

> Medical treatment was simply a physical manifestation of a change that had already happened. While transition is an important change, it was not the most profound one. Finding out who you are, resolving guilt and shame, confronting the past and starting to

---

22 Beardsley, 'The Transsexual person is my neighbour', p 16.
23 Chris Dowd, 'Five things cis folk don't know about trans folk because it isn't on trashy TV – my right of reply,' in Christina Beardsley and Michelle O'Brien (eds.), *This is my body* (London: DLT, 2016), p 102.
24 Dowd, 'Five things cis folk don't know', p 102.

envisage a better future are far more difficult and profound changes to personhood. The blade of a scalpel or a shot of artificial hormones can't do this.[25]

Furthermore, just as medical treatment was not the start of the process of change neither was it the end of it.

> Many of the folk I interviewed continued to heal psychologically and spiritually for many years after medical treatment concluded. Once freed, they were able to heal and create a new life. This wasn't a mechanistic medical process but rather a journey of identity. Sexuality needed to be explored and re-evaluated, previous relationships renegotiated, the past integrated and the wounds created by living a life with gender dysphoria needed to be healed. This is the work of years.[26]

Dowd notes that his research also showed that in the case of Christian trans folk transition was marked by a re-evaluation of their faith and forgiveness of themselves and others.

> My research showed an almost universal shift in religious outlook from a literalist and often narrow viewpoint to a much more expansive and generous view of God and others. A gentler, all-embracing and all loving deity replaced an angry Father God over the course of years. One of the striking findings of my research was the almost universality of forgiveness. Many of the interviewees spoke about a process of forgiving themselves and also forgiving others for the hurts incurred in the past. Many of the interviewees had recognised that the only way to completely free themselves of their pasts was through both extending and receiving forgiveness.[27]

He also notes that not all trans folk opt for surgical change. 'Some were happy to express their gender variance in non-medicalised ways or ways that did not require what we would see as full physical transition.'[28]

A second assumption that Dowd encountered was the idea that trans folk change their gender. Dowd rejects this assumption because:

> While I completely accept that some people transition physically I believe it is simply folk becoming who they are. What changes is the potential to express physically the spirit that already lives in a not

---

[25] Dowd, 'Five things cis folk don't know', p 102.
[26] Dowd, 'Five things cis folk don't know', p 103.
[27] Dowd, 'Five things cis folk don't know', p 103.
[28] Dowd, 'Five things cis folk don't know', p 103.

particularly satisfactory natal body. If the aim of the gender journey is to resolve this gender dissonance, it is logical to argue that the person and their preferred gender identity pre-exists. This means that trans folk don't change their gender but rather manifest their pre-existing but obscured gender.

While this may seem an excessively subtle point, I believe it is an important one. Recognising that the identity of trans folk pre-exists reframes their gender journey from becoming another identity to becoming fully themselves. This also takes out the idea that gender transition is a choice but simply a process of finding and claiming oneself. The only choice is between integrity of identity and continued disassociation from selfhood.[29]

A third assumption he encountered was that 'trans folk liked drawing attention to themselves.'[30] Dowd explains that his research showed him that the opposite was true. What he found was 'that trans folk often micromanaged their behaviours so that they did not draw attention to themselves.'[31] The people he encountered in the course of his research, he says:

> ...were not gender rebels. They did not want to overturn binary gender, create a radical theology or challenge church systems and structures. They simply wanted to be unremarkable people worshipping quietly in church communities which valued them as fellow Christians. Their greatest ambition was to blend in, not stand out.[32]

A fourth assumption was that 'trans folk are somehow unbiblical.' Dowd makes four responses to this assumption.

First, he looks at the prohibition of cross dressing in Deuteronomy 22:5 and suggests that a distinction needs to be made 'between someone who is wearing clothing appropriate to their identity and those who are not.' In his view 'trans folk not wearing clothing appropriate to their preferred gender are more likely to be in contravention of this prohibition than those who are.'[33]

In addition, he says: 'unless we took all the Deuteronomic prohibitions seriously, including prohibitions against tattoos, eating

---

29 Dowd, 'Five things cis folk don't know', p 104.
30 Dowd, 'Five things cis folk don't know', p 104.
31 Dowd, 'Five things cis folk don't know', p 104.
32 Dowd, 'Five things cis folk don't know', pp 104-105.
33 Dowd, 'Five things cis folk don't know', p 105.

shell fish, banking, poly cotton and Freudian therapy,' it is difficult to justify using the verse as a prohibition of transgender behaviour even if it is read literally.[34]

Secondly, he notes that the Bible contains lots of gender variant images:

> ...women are called brothers (Romans 14:10, 1 Corinthians 6:5-6). We are all brides of Christ (Ephesians 5:25-27), all part of the one body (Ephesians 5:30). Paul writes of himself as a woman giving birth (Galatians 4:19) and Galatians 3:28 asserts that there is no male or female but all are one in Christ Jesus.[35]

Thirdly he notes that appeal is made to the eunuchs who appear in the Bible in Esther, Isaiah, Matthew 19 and Acts 8. While accepting that eunuchs are biblical examples of 'gender variant folk' he is unhappy about identifying them with transgender people today because (a) they didn't have gender dysphoria, (b) they had power and influence while 'transfolk are some of the most socially and economically disadvantaged people in UK society' and (c) by equating 'mutilated genitals' with gender dysphoria such an identification 'places trans identity entirely in the physical.'[36]

Fourthly, Dowd contends that we can see a similarity between the experience of transgender people and the book of Job.

> Just as Job suffered the loss of his social position, family and 'very identity' so also trans folk have lost families, friends, homes and jobs and have encountered hostility and exclusion from churches and ministers.[37]

Just like 'Job's friends who gather round and speculate and blame, the few documents produced by the Church do the same thing.'[38] The two main documents, the Evangelical Alliance's *Transsexuality* and the Church of England's *Some Issues in Human Sexuality*:

> ...attempt to apply a rigid theological framework to explain something they do not understand, without once considering the problem is with the framework they are using and not the people they are discussing.[39]

---

34   Dowd, 'Five things cis folk don't know', p 105.
35   Dowd, 'Five things cis folk don't know', p 105.
36   Dowd, 'Five things cis folk don't know', p 105.
37   Dowd, 'Five things cis folk don't know', pp 105-106.
38   Dowd, 'Five things cis folk don't know', p 106.
39   Dowd, 'Five things cis folk don't know', p 106.

Just as Job consistently maintained his innocence so also many of the trans folk Dowd interviewed: 'continued to assert the integrity of their lives, and their belief that God had not only continued to journey with them, but that their own journeys were blessed.'[40]

Just as Job's story had a happy ending, so also many of those Dowd interviewed:

....felt that their lives were immeasurably better after coming out. Many had found the sense of peace and wholeness they had been seeking and that had prompted them to begin their gender journey. In the process they had engaged a deeper, more generous and engaged spirituality.[41]

In Dowd's view the Church can be seen to be like Job's friends in its approach to trans folk. Just as the book of Job:

...mocks the so-called wisdom of Job's accusers, and their clumsy theological ramblings about why Job has been afflicted, I believe that the Church, in its self-referential musings, is just as exposed. By creating theology that does not reflect on the experience of trans folk and take heed of those with professional knowledge working with them, the Church is not only being profoundly incurious but attempting to create theology based on assumptions, fears and prejudices that have little basis in reality.[42]

Finally, Dowd concludes his chapter by explaining why trans folk are not a threat to the Church, but instead have much to contribute to it:

While I acknowledge that rigid interpretation of Genesis becomes impossible, we gain so much from listening to the experiences of trans folk. The costly act of seeking to become the person that God intended us to be is seen as the aim of a Christian life. Few pay a greater cost then those trans folk in their seeking to follow God's special calling to them to integrity and wholeness. Few others have to continue to believe in a good and beneficent God (and indeed strengthen their faith) through such a time of testing. Few make enormous personal sacrifices to continue to belong to the Body of Christ even when it is refusing to hear or acknowledge the pain it has caused and remains mired in arrogance and wilful denial. And finally, trans folk show us that forgiveness of ourselves and others is the key to freeing ourselves from what binds us. These are powerful

---

40 Dowd, 'Five things cis folk don't know', p 106.
41 Dowd, 'Five things cis folk don't know', p 106.
42 Dowd, 'Five things cis folk don't know', pp 106-107.

and profound lessons for us all to learn. It is time for we cis folk to stop assuming and start listening. There is much to learn and so many wonderful people to meet.[43]

2.3. *Justin Tanis: Trans-Gendered, Theology, Ministry and Communities of Faith*

Justin Tanis' 2003 book *Trans-Gendered, Theology, Ministry and Communities of Faith* had its origins in his doctoral dissertation at San Francisco Theological Seminary. Tanis is transgendered and he explains that the purpose of his book is 'to delve into the spiritual nature of transgendered people, to hear the stories of others like me, and to give a positive voice to our community.'[44]

In his book Tanis argues that it is important to develop a transgendered understanding of God rather than seeing God in traditional masculine terms. He writes:

A transgendered image of God allows us to see God beyond binary categories. In fact, when gender is not emphasized first about God, it expands our ability to see other characteristics as more important than gender. After all, the gender of God does not make God divine. So much of human life is filtered through the lenses of 'is it a boy or a girl?' that we consciously or unconsciously use these same filters for God. The level of passion evoked by discussions of inclusive language shows the level of fear that surrounds the very question of God's gender. The gendered nature of language that has shifted so dramatically in our broader culture in the last fifty years or so has barely begun to change in our religious communities. Even in denominations like Metropolitan Community Church that have an official policy about inclusive language, for some people inclusive language is at best controversial and at worst seen as a sign of denigrating the divine.[45]

However, according to Tanis such linguistic conservatism is mistaken since:

...an intersexed or transgendered image of God, one that embodies both male and female, is more biblically accurate than one that

---

43 Dowd, 'Five things cis folk don't know', p 107.
44 Justin Tanis, *Trans-Gendered, Theology, Ministry and Communities of Faith* (Cleveland: Pilgrim Press, 2003), p 5.
45 Tanis, *Trans-Gendered*, p 137.

forces God into a single-gendered box. This image is also borne out by a study of other world religions in which the divine is seen in both feminine and masculine expressions. For transgendered and intersexed people then, we can look at ourselves and see ourselves in the divine image – what is true about us is also true about God and, conversely, the nature of God is also our nature.[46]

Expanding on this last point Tanis goes on to declare:

> The nature of God is to embody all genders, and thus it is natural for those of us who do as well. Rather than being outside of the divine order, intersexed and transgendered individuals are an integral part of creation, a creation that God declared was good.[47]

Tanis defends the idea of transgender as part of God's good creation in opposition to Oliver O'Donovan's argument that transsexualism is contrary to the natural order which God has established. Tanis writes:

> This planet teems with diverse forms of life. Vast differences exist between leaves, snowflakes, species, fur types and an infinite number of other things. That people can look at creation and see limitations rather than an ever-expanding array of difference is perplexing to me. If the Creator's will is expressed in the creation, then that will surely include a passion for variety and exultation in the beauty of differences. Intersexed and transgendered persons are, then, expressions of the natural order and should be upheld as part of the Creator's world.[48]

Summarising his argument about transgender and God, Tanis declares that transgendered people are:

> ...sacred because we are created in the image and likeness of God. Our sacred writings tell us that God knew us before even we were born and shaped us. God must have known of this transgendered being, because God was present when I was conceived and when I was born. God has been present through all I have experienced. And Scripture tells us that the Holy One saw what s/he had created and pronounced it good.[49]

---

46 Tanis, *Trans-Gendered*, p 137.
47 Tanis, *Trans-Gendered*, p 138.
48 Tanis, *Trans-Gendered*, p 143.
49 Tanis, *Trans-Gendered*, p 145.

As well as affirming that transgender people have been created by God and are for this reason sacred Tanis also contends that 'we have a responsibility for our own creation.' What he means by this is that:

> We are called to be artisans of our own lives and bodies. We should take responsibility for our own continued creation, both the development of our inner selves and our outer bodies. As trans people, we should take seriously the task of creating for ourselves the lives to which we feel called and compelled. We are shape shifters, finding ways to move from one way of being to another; some of us do this over and over again while others change once. When we see this process as sacred, we can claim our places as artist cooperating with God in creating the developing changing person that we are and that we are becoming.[50]

Two elements in this quotation that are very important for Tanis are the belief that human beings consist of inner selves or spirits and outer bodies and the notion of a way of life which God calls us to live.

On the former he writes:

> As trans people, we learn that both body and spirit are integral to our identities. We are bodies, and we are not only bodies. We discover that our bodies do not completely define us. The information that our bodies convey about us is relevant, but it is not the only perspective. This information is not all there is to know. We learn, too, how important it is that our bodies tell the truth about who we are and that we need our bodies to be congruent with our identities. Precisely because we value our bodies, we need them to express – through our bodies or our physical forms – what we know about ourselves. We love our bodies into new forms and new ways of moving in the world.

> At the same time, we are spirits but more than spirits. Our spirits speak to us, often from a very early age, of a reality that is in defiance of what we are told about ourselves. Those spirits define how we see ourselves. The self that develops within us is independent of the body and simultaneously longs to be one with it. We cannot have one without the other and be whole, healthy, human beings. Being united in body and spirit is our goal and our strength.[51]

---

50 Tanis, *Trans-Gendered*, p 182.
51 Tanis, *Trans-Gendered*, pp 183-184.

On the latter he states:

> To follow our callings as transgendered people means we need to make a shift in our lives. This shift may or may not mean action in terms of how we access medical technology to change our bodies, but it does mean taking ourselves and our genders seriously and acting to identify ourselves with who we are and who we are becoming. I do not believe that we can remain passive and still genuinely answer a calling. God calls us to move beyond our fears, beyond our doubts, and beyond the pressures of society and family to say 'yes' to true selves. That declaration is an act of faithful response to our calling.[52]

Turning to the Bible, Tanis holds that it can be read in a way that is supportive of transgender people.

He argues that the creation narrative in Genesis 1 tells us that God's act of creation:

> ...even while differentiating between elements of creation, still leaves space for 'in between' things: dusk, dawn, intersexed persons. God blesses all these parts of creation calling them Good.[53]

He further argues that in Genesis 2 male and female human beings are created out of an original androgynous earth creature. This passage, he writes, could be seen as:

> ...opening up the possibilities of gender. If completeness comes from having both male and female, than a person who possessed both is a return to the original completion in the earth creature.[54]

Moving on to Deuteronomy 22:5 he declares that 'the most compelling argument against this passage as a prohibition against cross-dressing is that we fail to follow any of the other directives around it.'[55] Contemporary faith communities, he says, are unconcerned 'about any of the blending of things cited in Deuteronomy other than the blending of male and female.'[56] Thus they do not prohibit the mixing of two types of seeds in a garden even though a literal reading of Deuteronomy

---

[52] Tanis, *Trans-Gendered*, p 158.
[53] Tanis, *Trans-Gendered*, p 59.
[54] Tanis, *Trans-Gendered*, p 61.
[55] Tanis, *Trans-Gendered*, p 66.
[56] Tanis, *Trans-Gendered*, p 66.

would forbid this. This shows 'that the concerns are about gender and very little about the need or desire to follow the dictates of ancient law.'[57]

In a similar fashion he notes that the exclusion from worship of someone whose testicles have been crushed or penis cut off commanded in Deuteronomy 23:1 is not applied to those 'who have lost their genitals because of accidents or illness.' It follows that 'to apply this passage also to transsexuals, while ignoring its implications for others, would be wrong.'[58] He also notes Sally Goss's argument that if taken literally this verse would seem to prohibit genital surgery on intersexed infants.

Tanis sees the welcome and inclusion of eunuchs in Isaiah 56:1-5 as relevant to transgendered people because:

> Eunuchs are the closest biblical analogy we have to transgendered people. Not only were eunuchs subject to physical modification through castration, but they also shifted roles in society from the clearly defined male and female gender roles.[59]

According to Tanis:

> For transgendered persons who have a sense of an internal reality that is or may be in conflict with our physical bodies, the prophet speaks a word that focuses on the faithfulness of our lives, not on the particularities of our bodies. God's emphasis is not on where our bodies came from or how they have been altered, but rather on the ways in which we practice our faith. Justice, inclusion and faithfulness become the primary indicators of people who are acceptable to God.[60]

Tanis sees Jesus' saying about eunuchs in Matthew 19:12 and the account of the Ethiopian eunuch in Acts 8:25-39 as further evidence of God's acceptance of transgendered people.

On Matthew 19:12 he writes:

> Clearly Jesus knows that some people are born outside the binary gender system and people whose lives lead them beyond it. He speaks of multiple ways in which someone might become gender variant, and he does so with compassion and clarity. We are called to do likewise.

---

[57] Tanis, *Trans-Gendered*, p 66.
[58] Tanis, *Trans-Gendered*, p 68.
[59] Tanis, *Trans-Gendered*, p 69.
[60] Tanis, *Trans-Gendered*, p 70.

Jesus goes on to acknowledge a connection between the dominion of God and eunuchs. We see in the words of Jesus an acceptance and acknowledgement of gender diversity. Modern science and medical knowledge support Jesus' concept that someone can become a eunuch in multiple ways, including being born intersexed and those who choose this status.[61]

On Acts 8:25-39 he writes:

Once again, we see an affirmation in Scripture that neither the gender of the eunuch nor his gender variance is pivotal to his inclusion or exclusion from the community of faith, but rather his desire to be baptized and included. Again, we see God's focus on faithfulness rather than physical characteristics. The categories in which society placed the eunuch were not God's categories and did not limit his access to the Divine. His willingness and his enthusiasm were the hallmarks of his conversation, not the external categories that surely controlled many of his other choices in life.[62]

Tanis further comments that the fact that 'this person is a eunuch is not erased or marginalized in the story.' This points us to the truth that 'God does not ask us to put aside who we are in order to be part of the community of faith, but rather calls us as we are in our specificity.'[63]

Finally, Tanis looks at the significance of St. Paul's teaching in Galatians 3:28 that 'There is no longer Jew or Greek, there is no longer slave or free, there is no longer male and female; for you are all one in Christ Jesus.' This teaching, he states:

...calls us to a unity that extends to all and provides us with a way of seeing one another, not as male or female, Jew or Greek, slave or free, but as Christians and children of God first and foremost. Rudy goes on to argue that if 'Christian' is the primary identity to which we are called, are the categories of male and female even useful? In fact, if the Christian community fulfils its mission to embrace all, as Rudy suggests, then, she says, 'surely gender is not the most interesting thing that can be said about each member [of the community].' This passage paints for us a vision of a world beyond gender, in which there is room for infinite variety and infinite grace.'[64]

---

61 Tanis, *Trans-Gendered*, p 75.
62 Tanis, *Trans-Gendered*, p 79.
63 Tanis, *Trans-Gendered*, p 79.
64 Tanis, *Trans-Gendered*, p 83 quoting Kathy Ruby, *Sex and the Church* (Boston: Beacon Press, 1997), p 100.

Tanis' overall conclusion about the biblical material is that 'the Scriptures are ours as much as they are anyone's.'[65] In his view:

> The texts that some religious people use to condemn us show that even in biblical times gender-variant people were living in communities of faith and striving to find their place within society and before God. We have been a part of the story of the Bible from the earliest days, from the inter-sexed origins of Adam, to the cross-dressing Israelites in the times that the law was set out in Deuteronomy, to the eunuchs, to a vision of a world and a community beyond the bounds of male and female. To me, seeing the record of our ancestors there at all, is affirming and amazing, but we are there.[66]

Alongside his development of a transgender affirming reading of the Bible Tanis also develops a transgender affirming account of the significance of Jesus, what he calls a 'Trans Christology.'

Tanis notes, but is unconvinced by, the argument put forward by Mollenkott and others that if Jesus was born of a virgin he would have been intersex since he would have had female chromosomes even if he had a male body. He argues instead that the significance of Jesus for transgender people lies in the way in which he was 'queer' and in the fact that he was someone who went through a process of transition.

For Tanis the queerness of Jesus consists in the way in which:

> ...he differed from that which was expected and sanctioned by his society and the religious leaders of the day. We can never know if Jesus himself was intersexed, but we do see the record of his ministry and the way in which he challenged people to a radically inclusive view of the world and of the holy. We see how queerly he interacted with religious authorities and ordinary people, in ways that shocked, challenged and transformed them. Some left his presence scandalized while others followed filled with hope and a new vision of their lives and their world. The same is true today. The queer Christ is shocking to some and liberating to others, and, at best, we can allow ourselves to be both shocked and freed, to be challenged and to be comforted, to be human and holy.[67]

On Jesus and transition he observes:

---

[65] Tanis, *Trans-Gendered*, p 84.
[66] Tanis, *Trans-Gendered*, p 84.
[67] Tanis, *Trans-Gendered*, pp 141-142.

Jesus himself undergoes a remarkable process of transition through his death and resurrection. He is transformed in his life through his encounters with others, is transfigured on the mountaintop, and finally is transformed through death from the living Jesus to the resurrected Christ, who is unrecognizable to those who knew him until he reveals himself. Within his body, he contains both finite life and eternal life, both death and resurrection, in the way that transgendered people embody both male and female. The holiness of Christ is that he is both/and, both human and divine, both mortal and eternal.

When we are baptized, we are baptized into this changing, transformational Christ, who rises above human limitations of gender, class and nation, as Paul declares in Galatians 3:28. We are called beyond human limitations to be participants in the realm of God, a dominion of peace and justice.[68]

As Tanis sees it, the transformation undergone by Jesus also provides us with a healthy way of looking at the transformation undergone by transgendered people who transition.

Jesus' body was changed, both by becoming alive after death and in ways that made him appear different to those who knew him; at the same time, he was the same Jesus who had been among them, as Jesus' revelation to Thomas shows us. Here Jesus is careful to make the point that he is both the same and different, which is true of us as well. Jesus did not die and return as a wholly different being but a transfigured and resurrected one. In this way, Jesus is a trans person. Both through his personal transformations in body and spirit, and in the ways in which he embodies, transcends and defies categorization.[69]

A chapter of Tanis' book is concerned with a variety of ways in which religious communities can created a 'genuine welcome' for transgender people in accordance with the way in which they are welcomed by God. Among these ways is the provision of the kind of rites envisaged in the Blackburn motion.

One important way to serve the trans community is to ritually mark the changes that are occurring in their lives and to have the community's prayers and blessings. Having a service to celebrate and bless a change in name, which acts as a public pronouncement

---

[68] Tanis, *Trans-Gendered*, p 142.
[69] Tanis, *Trans-Gendered*, pp 142-143.

of the name, and of the transition, adds considerable meaning to a person's transition. Such a service recognizes the event spiritually and allows the community to witness and bless this milestone. Depending on the community's understanding of baptism, this service may include a reaffirmation of the baptismal covenant or a rebaptism with a new name. The faith community needs to put the word out to trans folks that this option is available in your place of worship; people may not be aware that a church or synagogue will offer this type of ritual.[70]

2.4. An overview of the arguments put forward by Beardsley, Dowd and Tanis.

Beardsley, Dowd and Tanis do not say exactly the same thing. However, what they say overlaps and we can put together their arguments to present a composite argument for the acceptance of gender transition and for having a rite to mark this that reflects the sort of approach that is generally taken by those who are supportive of gender transition. This composite argument would run as follows.

Because God has both male and female aspects we should view God as being transgender or intersex.

God has created transgender people as part of the variety of his creation. Such people are ordinary people who have a self or spirit that is of one sex and a body that is another. All they want to do is to live as the people God made them to be and in order to do this they have to give expression to the sex of their self or spirit. This means that it is right not only to declare who they truly are, but to seek to adjust their bodies through the use of hormones and surgery so that it expresses this sex more adequately.

Science and medicine support this idea of transition. Science teaches us that the sense that transgender people have that they belong to a particular sex has a biological basis in the nature of their brains and medicine tells us that it is appropriate to treat the psychological distress that transgender people experience through the use of hormones and sex-reassignment surgery.

This view of the existence of transgender people is compatible with the teaching of the creation narratives in Genesis 1 and 2 and is supported by the way in which the Bible gives a welcome to eunuchs in

---

70 Tanis, *Trans-Gendered*, p 143.

Isaiah 56:1-5, Matthew 19:10-12 and Acts 8:26-40. Further biblical support for transgender people is provided by the way in which the Bible uses gender variant language to describe the Church and teaches in Galatians 3:28 that in Christ there is neither male nor female and by the biblical themes of the transformation of creation, of death and resurrection and of people receiving a new name. The prohibition of cross-dressing in Deuteronomy 22:5 is not relevant to the current debate about transgender issues.

Jesus can be seen as a model for transgender people in a variety of ways. Some have argued that Jesus' virgin birth means that he was intersex in that he must have had female chromosomes even if he had a male body. Others have found inspiration in the fact that Jesus was someone who was 'queer' in the sense that he was someone who went against the conventional expectations of his society, and in the way in which Jesus himself went through a process of transition while remaining the same person and combined both humanity and divinity and death and resurrection in the same way that transgender people embody both male and female.

The calling of those in the Church is not to be like Job's comforters, criticising other people's suffering while being ignorant of what is really going on. They need instead to offer transgender people love, acceptance and support, accepting that transgender people are learning to love themselves so that they are then better equipped to love others. They also need to learn from transgender Christians who model what it means to journey towards wholeness and integrity in faithfulness to God's call at great personal cost.

Offering a rite to mark gender transition is an important way for the Church to affirm transgender people and the journey they have undertaken.

In the next chapter we shall undertake a critical examination of these ideas.

3. A critical examination of the case for the acceptance of gender transition

3.1. Is God transgender or intersex?

The claim that God should be seen as being transgender or intersex has two problems.

The first problem is that of relevance. This is because even if it could be shown that God is transgender or intersex this would not mean that being transgender or intersex was a good thing for human beings. How God is, is not necessarily how human beings are meant to be.

Thus God is omnipresent and omniscient, but this is not how God has made human beings, who exist in limited points in space and are limited in their knowledge. Similarly, God could be transgender or intersex and he could nevertheless have created human beings to be clearly either male or female.

The second problem is that the claim that God is in fact transgender or intersex is difficult to sustain. It is true that Scripture uses both male and female language to refer to God. Thus on the one hand God is referred to by the male images of a father (Psalm 103:13), a husband (Hosea 2:16) and a king (Psalm 98:6) and on the other hand he is referred to by the female images of a pregnant woman (Isaiah 42:14), a mother (Isaiah 66:13) and a midwife (Psalm 22:9). However, it would be a mistake to assume from this imagery that God is a mixture of male and female and thus can be seen as transgender or intersex.

This is because such language is analogical rather than literal. God is no more literally a father or a mother in a human sexual sense than he is literally a shepherd (Psalm 23:1), a rock (Psalm 18:2) or a lion (Hosea 13:8). Rather, God is in some specific non sexual ways like a human father or mother just as God is in some specific ways like a shepherd, a rock or a lion.

In her book *The New Eve in Christ* Mary Hayter notes that 'a growing number of feminists teach that the God/ess combines male and female characteristics' and warns that 'They, like those who assume that God is exclusively male, should remember that any attribution of sexuality to God is a reversion to paganism.'[1] As she goes on to say:

> The masculine terminology does not denote a male deity; the feminine terminology does not denote a female deity; nor does the mixture of masculine and feminine terminology denote an androgynous God/ess. Rather, the indications are that the God of the Bible uniquely incorporates and transcends all sexuality. As Sapp puts it: 'The distinction between the sexes is a creation by God since there is no such distinction on the divine level; the polarity of the sexes belongs to the created order and not to God.'
>
> Neither male nor female sexuality can be ascribed to Yahweh, for the limitations which characterize mankind do not affect the sovereign transcendence of God (cf. Isaiah 40:25).[2]

This criticism of some forms of feminist theology applies equally to those theologians who want to say that God is transgender or intersex. They, too, are forgetting the basic theological rule of the utter transcendence of God and the necessary limitations of human language when referring to God. The transcendent creator God does not have sex as his creatures do and therefore it makes no sense to say that God is transgender or intersex. There is nothing that we know about God that suggests that he experiences conflict between his inner self and the sex of his body as transgender people do, or that he has ambiguous sexual characteristics as intersex people do.

3.2.   Are people created by God to be transgender?

It is a basic axiom of Christian theology that all that exists does so because God wills it. However, this does not mean that it is right to say that everything that exists is part of the creation that is described as good in the book of Genesis. There are some parts of the created order that are not as they should be.

If we focus on God's human creation we can see, for example, that although God created human beings to be seeing creatures there are some people who are blind, that although God created human beings to walk there are some people who are lame and that although God created

---

[1]   Mary Hayter, *The New Eve in Christ* (London: SPCK, 1987), p 41.

[2]   Hayter, *The New Eve in Christ* p 41 quoting Stephen Sapp, *Sexuality, the Bible and Science* (Philadelphia: Fortress Press, 1977), p 3.

human beings to be mentally healthy there are some people who suffer from mental illness.

The question with regard to transgender people is whether they are an example of the variety that God wills for his human creatures, as would be true, for instance, of differences of hair colour or skin colour, or whether they are examples of something that is not as it should be, as in the case of the examples in the previous paragraph.

The starting point for answering this question is the observation that both Scripture and science teach us that the human race is, in the words of Oliver O'Donovan, 'sexually dimorphic and heterosexually procreative.'[3] That is to say, God has created human beings as embodied creatures, who have two physically distinct forms, known in English as male and female, which are oriented to the propagation of children through sexual intercourse. This basic, God given, biological distinction between male and female human beings is the basis upon which human societies have created patterns of gender differentiation which govern how male and female human beings are expected to behave and relate to each other.

As we have noted earlier in this paper, transgender people feel that there is an incongruity between who they truly are and the sex of their physical embodiment. This causes them acute mental distress which they seek to overcome through declaring their true identity, seeking to live according to that identity and changing their bodies so that they more adequately express that identity.

The existence of this sense of incongruity can be seen as a clear indication that in the case of transgender people things are not as they should be. The Christian belief in the goodness of God must lead us to believe that God did not create people with the intention that they should have this sense of incongruity. People should be able to accept and indeed rejoice in their particular physical embodiment as male or female as a good gift from God and fact that transgender people cannot do this is indicative that something has gone wrong in the course of their development. In Christian theological terms the existence of transgender people is a result of the brokenness of a fallen world in the same way that conditions such as blindness, lameness and mental illness are.

---

[3]   Oliver O'Donovan, *Transsexualism: Issues and Argument* (Cambridge: Grove Books, 2007), p 6.

The conclusion that something has gone wrong in the course of the development of a transgender person does not, of course, settle the question of what has gone wrong. It could be that the problem lies with the development of their body, which is not able to properly express who they truly are. On the other hand, it could be that the problem lies in their mind which has developed in such a way that is unable to accept the sex of their body. We shall return to this issue of where the problem lies, but for the moment we can simply accept that a problem exists. Something is wrong.

3.3. Is transgender a matter of the biology of the brain?

One explanation for the existence of transgender people that has come to the fore in recent years is the idea that transgender is a matter of the biology of the brain, an idea which we have seen referred to by Beardsley in the previous chapter. This idea modifies the normal claim that transgender is a matter of a person's self-perception versus the reality of the nature of their body. It holds instead that a transgender person is someone who has a brain that corresponds to their preferred sex rather than to the sex of the rest of their physical body. They think they are female even though they have a predominantly male body and vice versa because the way that their brain has developed means that is what their brain is telling them. In simplified terms what is proposed is that there are people with a male body and a female brain and other people with a female body and a male brain.

This is now what is being taught in schools. A supply teacher for example, records the kind of material she was given for lessons on transgender:

> The three lessons I was asked to deliver were like something from the 50s in terms of gender stereotypes. Slick animations showed diagrams of boys with mainly blue brains and girls with mainly pink brains. Amongst these pink and blue-brained figures were a minority of boys with pink brains and girls with blue brains. A video interview with a doctor explained that sometimes biology gets it wrong and a boy or a girl will be born with the "wrong" brain in the "wrong" body. But, now it is all ok because medical science can "fix" this and put the right brain in the right body.[4]

---

4   Quoted in 'Teaching Transgender Doctrine In Schools – A Bizarre Educational Experiment' at http://www.transgendertrend.com/teaching-transgender-doctrine-in-schools-a-bizarre-educational-experiment/

For those supportive of gender transition the great strength of this understanding of transgender is that it appears to give scientific backing to what transgender people believe about themselves. They are not mistaken in thinking that there is an incongruity between their sense of self and their predominant biology. They think this way because the biology of their brain really is that of their preferred sex. Transgender is thus not the result of the mind versus biology. It is instead a matter of the mind reflecting a person's divided biology and since the biology of the brain is what determines a person's sense of self it is better to go with what it is saying.

However, there is a major problem with this understanding of transgender, which is that the available scientific evidence does not seem to support it. Thus after surveying the relevant research in the field of neurobiology (the biology of the brain), Lawrence Meyer and Paul McHugh note that:

> ...it remains unclear whether and to what extent neurobiological findings say anything meaningful about gender identity. It is important to note that regardless of their findings, studies of this kind cannot support any conclusion that individuals come to identify as a gender that does not correspond to their biological sex because of an innate, biological condition of the brain.
>
> The question is not simply whether there are differences between the brains of transgender individuals and people identifying with the gender corresponding to their biological sex, but whether gender identity is a fixed, innate, and biological trait, even when it does not correspond to biological sex, or whether environmental or psychological causes contribute to the development of a sense of gender identity in such cases. Neurological differences in transgender adults might be the consequence of biological factors such as genes or prenatal hormone exposure, or of psychological and environmental factors ... or they could result from some combination of the two. There are no serial, longitudinal, or prospective studies looking at the brains of cross-gender identifying children who develop to later identify as transgender adults. Lack of this research severely limits our ability to understand causal relationships between brain morphology, or functional activity, and the later development of gender identity different from biological sex.[5]

---

[5] Lawrence Meyer and Paul McHugh, 'Gender Identity' in *New Atlantis*, Fall 2016, p 102.

Furthermore, they say,

> ...it is now widely recognized among psychiatrists and neuroscientists who engage in brain imaging research that there are inherent and ineradicable methodological limitations of any neuroimaging study that simply associates a particular trait, such as a certain behavior, with a particular brain morphology. (And when the trait in question is not a concrete behavior but something as elusive and vague as 'gender identity,' these methodological problems are even more serious.) These studies cannot provide statistical evidence nor show a plausible biological mechanism strong enough to support causal connections between a brain feature and the trait, behavior, or symptom in question.[6]

Their overall conclusion is that:

> In short, the current studies on associations between brain structure and transgender identity are small, methodologically limited, inconclusive, and sometimes contradictory. Even if they were more methodologically reliable, they would be insufficient to demonstrate that brain structure is a cause, rather than an effect, of the gender-identity behavior.[7]

At the moment, therefore, we cannot say that science shows us that transgender people suffer from gender dysphoria because of the biology of their brains. As Mark Yarhouse writes, the reality is that 'We don't know what causes gender dysphoria.'[8] We know that things are not as they should be, but we don't know why.

3.4. What is the best way to resolve the distress felt by transgendered people?

As we have seen, it is argued by transgender advocates that the best way to resolve the distress felt by transgendered people is for them to accept who they truly are and to live this out combined with medical intervention to bring their bodies into greater conformity with their true identity. As we have also seen, this view of the matter is now what is being taught in schools.

---

6   Meyer and McHugh, 'Gender Identity', p 103.
7   Meyer and McHugh, 'Gender Identity', p 104.
8   Mark Yarhouse, *Understanding Gender Dysphoria* (Downers Grove: IVP Academic, 2015), p 79.

Lying behind this view of the best way for transgendered people to overcome their distress are three convictions.

The first is the conviction that the true self of the transgendered person is something that is to be determined on the basis of the conviction of the person concerned. Given that studies of the brain are, as has been noted, inconclusive, there is no evidence for the preferred identity of a transgender person other than what they say about themselves.

The second is the conviction that personal sexual identity can be separated from the sex of the body. In the vast majority of cases there is no ambiguity about the physical sex of a transgender person. They are clearly and unambiguously physically either male or female. However, the claim made by the transgender person is that this physical identity does not correspond to their true self.

The third is the conviction that accepting and living as their true self and undergoing medical intervention is the best way for those who are transgender to resolve the distress they feel and become more whole people.

All three of these convictions raise problems.

The first conviction raises the obvious question as to why we should accept what transgender people say about their identity. This is because we do not automatically accept what people say about who they are when the evidence seems to point in another direction.

For example, the claim made by the American Civil Rights activist Rachel Dolezal that she is black has generally been rejected because she was born to white parents. Her argument, 'I acknowledge that I was biologically born white to white parents, but I identify as black'[9] has not been regarded as persuasive on the grounds that biology is determinative in the matter. Someone who is born of white parents is not black even if they self-identify as being so.

For another example, a young Norwegian girl called 'Nano' claims to be a cat trapped in the wrong body. According to the report in the *New York Daily News*:

A Norwegian woman claims she was 'born in the wrong species' and believes she is a cat trapped in a human's body. The 20-year-old known as Nano said she possesses a slew of catty characteristics like ultra-sharp hearing, laser night vision and fierce aversions to both

---

9   Sam Frizell, 'Rachel Dolezal: I Was Born White', *Time,* November 2, 2015.

dogs and water. 'It's also obvious that I'm a cat when I start purring and meowing,' she said in a YouTube video that has racked up more than 300,000 views. 'And walking around on four legs and stuff like that.' Nano said she first realized she was a cat when she was 16 years old. Doctors found a 'genetic defect' in her DNA, she said – which she believes proves she is a cat. 'Born in the wrong species,' she said. 'My psychologist told me I can grow out of it, but I doubt it.' The 20-year-old did not elaborate on the 'defect' or provide any proof that her DNA matches that of a cat. She looks entirely human, but she wears a cat-ear headband and a fluffy stuffed tail to help her inner feline match her outward appearance.[10]

As in the case of Rachel Dolezal, Nano's claim about her identity has not been accepted on the grounds that whatever she says she is, or believes about herself, she is biologically human rather than feline.

If in these two cases the claim that is being made is generally seen as untrue on the grounds that biological evidence trumps self-identification, it is not clear on what grounds it is argued that a similar claim should be accepted in the case of someone who is transgender. If, as noted previously in this paper, the basic distinction between men and women, on which all other distinctions between them depend, is a biological one, on what grounds can it be said that someone who is biologically male is female or vice versa?

A response that could be made to this question would be to appeal to the second conviction noted above, namely that someone can have a self whose identity is distinct from the biology of the body in which they exist. However, there are two problems with this conviction.

The first problem is that human beings are so made that a person's body is an integral part of who they are. It is part of their self. We can see this, for example, when someone says to an assailant 'you hit me.' What was hit was someone's body, but in hitting their body the assailant hit them. We can also see it if we consider the process of thought. While it can be coherently argued that thinking is an activity of the non-corporeal soul[11] it is (in this life at least) also an activity that involves biological processes (which is why it can be prevented by illness or accident). It is the whole self, body and soul together, that thinks.

---

10   New York Daily News, 'SEE IT: Norwegian woman believes she is a cat trapped in a human's body' at http://www.nydailynews.com/news/world/norwegian-woman-cat-trapped-human-body-article-1.2512352

11   See for instance J P Moreland, *The Soul: How we know it's real and why it matters* (Chicago: Moody Press, 2014).

This last point means that in the case of a transgender person one has the problematic concept of a self that can think *because* it has a male body thinking that it is not male, or conversely a self that can think *because* it has a female body thinking that it is not female. Arguably the nature of the thinking that is taking place is a denial of what is being thought.

The second problem is that it is not clear that it is coherent to think of a disembodied human self being male or female. As we have noted before, being male or female is before all else a biological distinction. However, a disembodied self has no body which has either male or female biology. How then can it be either male or female?

Nevertheless, this is what is being claimed in the case of a transgendered person. What is said is that a transgendered person is a self who is either male or female. However, their sex cannot be derived from the sex of the body in which that self is embodied since that is a body of the opposite sex. Yet there is no other body possessed by that self. So where does the sexual identity of that self come from? On what is based?

What all this means is that is unclear how it actually makes any sense to think of a self that has a different sex from its body. The basic claim made about transgender people thus seems to be incoherent.

The fact that the first two convictions are problematic means that the third conviction is also problematic. The idea that a transgender person needs to accept and live as their true self is based on the belief that their true self has a sex which is different from that of their body. As we have just seen, it is difficult to make sense of this claim.

It could, perhaps be argued that even if this claim does not make any sense transgender people should none the less be encouraged to live according to their desired sex and to adjust their bodies accordingly through the use of hormones and surgery because although their sense of sexual identity is illusory it nevertheless exists and they will be happier if they live as if it were true.

However, there have been a number of studies that call into question the assumption that going down this route does in fact succeed in giving people long term well-being.

For example a 2004 study by Birmingham University's Aggressive Research Intelligence Facility (Arif) assessed the findings of more than one hundred follow-up studies of post-operative transsexuals. An article in *The Guardian* summarized the findings of this research as follows:

Arif...concludes that none of the studies provides conclusive evidence that gender reassignment is beneficial for patients. It found that most research was poorly designed, which skewed the results in favour of physically changing sex. There was no evaluation of whether other treatments, such as long-term counselling, might help transsexuals, or whether their gender confusion might lessen over time. Arif says the findings of the few studies that have tracked significant numbers of patients over several years were flawed because the researchers lost track of at least half of the participants. The potential complications of hormones and genital surgery, which include deep vein thrombosis and incontinence respectively, have not been thoroughly investigated, either. 'There is huge uncertainty over whether changing someone's sex is a good or a bad thing,' says Dr Chris Hyde, director of Arif. 'While no doubt great care is taken to ensure that appropriate patients undergo gender reassignment, there's still a large number of people who have the surgery but remain traumatized – often to the point of committing suicide.'[12]

For a second example, a major study undertaken by a team from the Karolinska Institute and Gothenburg University in Sweden led by Cecilia Dhejne and published in 2011 looked at the long term outcomes for people who had undergone sex-reassignment surgery. This study compared a total of 324 people who underwent sex reassignment between 1973 and 2003 to two age-matched control groups, people of the same sex as the transsexual person at birth, and people of the sex to which the individual had been reassigned.

The study found:

...substantially higher rates of overall mortality, death from cardiovascular disease and suicide, suicide attempts, and psychiatric hospitalisations in sex-reassigned transsexual individuals compared to a healthy control population. This highlights that post-surgical transsexuals are a risk group that need long-term psychiatric and somatic follow-up. Even though surgery and hormonal therapy alleviates gender dysphoria, it is apparently not sufficient to remedy the high rates of morbidity and mortality found among transsexual persons.[13]

---

[12] David Batty, 'Mistaken identity,' *The Guardian,* July 30, 2004, http://www.theguardian.com/society/2004/jul/31/health.socialcare.

[13] Cecilia Djehne et al, 'Long-Term Follow-Up of Transsexual Persons Undergoing Sex Reassignment Surgery: Cohort Study in Sweden,' *PLoS One,* 6 (No.2), 2011, text at http://journals.plos.org/plosone/article?id=10.1371/journal.pone.0016885#s3

For a third example, the biggest ever survey of transgender people in the United States indicates that there is a far higher prevalence of mental and physical health issues among transgender people than among the population as whole.

The survey, undertaken by the National Center for Transgender Equality, surveyed 27,715 self-described transgender people in the United States in 2015. Key findings were that:

o   39% of transgender people had suffered serious recent psychological stress (as compared to 5% among Americans generally);

o   40% of transgender people had attempted suicide (as compared to 4.6% among Americans in general);

o   7% of transgender people had attempted suicide in the last year (as compared to 0.6% among Americans in general);

o   1.4% of transgender people were infected with HIV (as compared to 0.3% among Americans in general. In particular, 3.4% of male to female transsexuals and 19% of black male to female transsexuals had HIV.[14]

The 2015 survey does not distinguish between pre- and post-operative transsexuals, but together with the other two surveys and similar data from other surveys[15] its findings point us to the truth that being transgender is associated with serious issues of mental and physical well-being which often continue after transition has taken place.

In the words of Meyer and McHugh in their article previously cited:

> The scientific evidence summarized suggests we take a skeptical view toward the claim that sex-reassignment procedures provide the hoped for benefits or resolve the underlying issues that contribute to elevated mental health risks among the transgender population. While we work to stop maltreatment and misunderstanding, we should also work to study and understand whatever factors may contribute to the high rates of suicide and other psychological and behavioral health problems among the transgender population, and to think more clearly about the treatment options that are available.[16]

---

[14]   James, S. E., Herman, J. L., Rankin, S., Keisling, M., Mottet, L., & Anafi, M, *The Report of the 2015 U.S. Transgender Survey* (Washington, DC: National Center for Transgender Equality, 2016).

[15]   See Meyer and McHugh, 'Gender Identity', pp 109-113.

[16]   Meyer and McHugh, 'Gender Identity', p 113.

Another related issue which needs to be considered is the issue of 'de-transitioning,' that is, the issue of people who have gone through transition and afterwards revert to living according to their biological gender.

Two examples of de-transitioning are given, for instance, in an article published in August last year entitled 'Real-Life Victims of the Transgender 'Cult'.' The article runs as follows:

> More and more parents are stepping out, admitting that their children 'identify as transgender' and wanting to do something about it. Schools encourage gender confusion, and doctors reportedly won't even run preliminary tests if a child asks for life-altering 'treatment.' But before you sign your kids up, listen to the real-life stories of people who deeply regret their 'transition.'

> 'I am a real, live 22-year-old woman, with a scarred chest and a broken voice, and five o'clock shadow because I couldn't face the idea of growing up to be a woman, that's my reality,' admitted Cari Stella in a deeply personal YouTube video. She objected to transgender journalist Julia Serano's insistence on calling her 'transgender.'

> 'Gender was done to me, gender was traumatizing to me, I don't want anything to do with it anymore,' Stella declared. She admitted that 'when I was transitioning, I felt a strong desire – what I would have called a 'need' at the time – to transition,' but her transition only hurt her more. 'It can be damn hard to figure out that the treatment you're being told is to help you is actually making your mental health worse. Testosterone made me even more dissociated than I already was,' she said.

> Another de-transitioning woman, Carey Callahan, accused Serano of 'erasing' her, by insisting that because people like Callahan had transitioned, they were still transgender. 'If self-definition is a human right, I don't know how much louder we can shout to the world we're not trans,' Callahan said. 'And for me, if you say that I'm on the transgender spectrum, what you're doing is you're erasing everything I'm telling you about my life and my story.'

> 'I had trauma that led to me disassociating from my female body, and ... the longer I chased that disassociation – the more I asked people to call me special pronouns, the more I tried to change my body, the more I ensconced myself in a community that would affirm a trans identity, the worse I felt,' Callahan admitted.

She argued that Serano's insistence that people like her are still transgender is unfair and dishonest. 'It's a central story in my life, and you're erasing it to make me fit into your ideology.' Callahan added, 'Your set of ideas of how the world works is not worth acting like I don't exist, or acting like you get to define my gender for me. No, that's not how that works. I'm a real person, and you have to deal with my existence.'[17]

Another example is provided by the testimony of the Christian writer Walt Heyer. He explains how, 'overcome by the persistent feeling I was really a woman' he underwent sex-reassignment surgery:

> I sought out a prominent gender psychologist for evaluation, and he quickly assured me that I obviously suffered from gender dysphoria. A gender change, he told me, was the cure. Feeling that I had nothing to lose and thrilled that I could finally attain my lifelong dream, I underwent a surgical change at the age of forty-two. My new identity as Laura Jensen, female, was legally affirmed on my birth record, Social Security card, and driver's license. I was now a woman in everyone's eyes.
>
> The gender conflict seemed to fade away, and I was generally happy for a while.[18]

However, he says, the happiness was only temporary:

> I knew I wasn't a real woman, no matter what my identification documents said. I had taken extreme steps to resolve my gender conflict, but changing genders hadn't worked. It was obviously a masquerade. I felt I had been lied to. How in the world had I reached this point? How did I become a fake woman? I went to another gender psychologist, and she assured me that I would be fine; I just needed to give my new identity as Laura more time. I had a past, a battered and broken life that living as Laura did nothing to dismiss or resolve. Feeling lost and depressed, I drank heavily and considered suicide.
>
> At the three-year mark of life as Laura, my excessive drinking brought me to a new low. At my lowest point, instead of committing suicide I sought help at an alcohol recovery meeting. My sponsor, a

---

[17] Tyler O Neil, 'Real life victims of the transgender 'cult,' *P J Media*, August 21, 2016, Article at https://pjmedia.com/parenting/2016/08/21/real-life-victims-of-the-transgender-cult/

[18] Walt Heyer, 'I was a Transgender Woman,' *Public Discourse*, 1 April, 2015, article at http://www.thepublicdiscourse.com/2015/04/14688/

lifeline of support and accountability, mentored me in how to live life free from alcohol.

Sobriety was the first of several turning points in my transgender life.

As Laura, I entered a two-year university program to study the psychology of substance and alcohol abuse. I achieved higher grades than my classmates, many of whom had PhDs. Still, I struggled with my gender identity. It was all so puzzling. What was the point of changing genders if not to resolve the conflict? After eight years of living as a woman, I had no lasting peace. My gender confusion only seemed to worsen.

During an internship in a psychiatric hospital, I worked alongside a medical doctor on a lock-down unit. After some observation, he took me aside and told me I showed signs of having a dissociative disorder. Was he right? Had he found the key that would unlock a childhood lost? Rather than going to gender-change activist psychologists like the one who had approved me for surgery, I sought the opinions of several "regular" psychologists and psychiatrists who did not see all gender disorders as transgender. They agreed: I fit the criteria for dissociative disorder.

It was maddening. Now it was apparent that I had developed a dissociative disorder in childhood to escape the trauma of the repeated cross-dressing by my grandmother and the sexual abuse by my uncle. That should have been diagnosed and treated with psychotherapy. Instead, the gender specialist never considered my difficult childhood or even my alcoholism and saw only transgender identity. It was a quick jump to prescribe hormones and irreversible surgery. Years later, when I confronted that psychologist, he admitted that he should not have approved me for surgery.

Coming back to wholeness as a man after undergoing unnecessary gender surgery and living life legally and socially as a woman for years wasn't going to be easy. I had to admit to myself that going to a gender specialist when I first had issues had been a big mistake. I had to live with the reality that body parts were gone. My full genitalia could not be restored – a sad consequence of using surgery to treat psychological illness. Intensive psychotherapy would be required to resolve the dissociative disorder that started as a child.

But I had a firm foundation on which to begin my journey to restoration. I was living a life free from drugs and alcohol, and I was ready to become the man I was intended to be.

At age fifty-six, I experienced something beyond my wildest dreams. I fell in love, married, and began to fully re-experience life as a man. It took over fifty years, but I was finally able to unwind all the damage that purple chiffon dress had done. Today, I'm seventy-four years old and married to my wife of eighteen years, with twenty-nine years of sober living.[19]

The figure normally cited for those who regret having had sex-change surgery is 2% but the Arif survey cited above refers to research from America and the Netherlands which give figures for regret as high as 20% and as the debate about the transgender issue intensifies there is an increasing amount of testimony from people who have de-transitioned. Like the research into the mental and physical health of transgender people previously referred to, the testimony of those who have de-transitioned calls into question the claim that going through transition will necessarily bring about the release from mental anguish that is the goal of the process.

It is true that at the moment there is widespread support for transition as an appropriate solution for gender dysphoria among the members of the medical profession working in this field. However, two things need to be borne in mind.

The first is that the fact there is widespread support for a particular form of treatment does not mean that that form of treatment is correct. There are plenty of examples of forms of medical treatment that had widespread support in the past, but are now seen to be incorrect. Thus Heyer notes that in the twentieth century there was widespread medical and media support for lobotomies and other forms of surgical intervention as the best ways to treat mental illness, but today these forms of treatment are regarded as tragically mistaken.[20]

The second is that there are members of the medical profession with expert knowledge in the field of gender dysphoria who regard gender transition as the wrong form of treatment for this condition. A good example of this sort of informed dissent is the article 'Transgenderism: A Pathogenic Meme' by Paul McHugh. In this article he writes:

For forty years as the University Distinguished Service Professor of

---

19 Heyer, 'I was a Transgender Woman'. Heyer's full story can be found in his book *A Transgender's Faith* (Walt Heyer, 2015) and numerous other articles about de-transitioning can be found on his web site 'Sex Change Regret' at http://www.sexchangeregret.com/

20 Walter Heyer, *Paper Genders* (Make Waves Publishing, 2011).

Psychiatry at Johns Hopkins Medical School – twenty-six of which were also spent as Psychiatrist in Chief of Johns Hopkins Hospital – I've been studying people who claim to be transgender. Over that time, I've watched the phenomenon change and expand in remarkable ways.

A rare issue of a few men – both homosexual and heterosexual men, including some who sought sex-change surgery because they were erotically aroused by the thought or image of themselves as women – has spread to include women as well as men. Even young boys and girls have begun to present themselves as of the opposite sex. Over the last ten or fifteen years, this phenomenon has increased in prevalence, seemingly exponentially. Now, almost everyone has heard of or met such a person.

Publicity, especially from early examples such as 'Christine' Jorgenson, 'Jan' Morris, and 'Renee' Richards, has promoted the idea that one's biological sex is a choice, leading to widespread cultural acceptance of the concept. And, that idea, quickly accepted in the 1980s, has since run through the American public like a revelation or "meme" affecting much of our thought about sex.[21]

However, he argues, we need to address:

...the basic assumption of the contemporary parade: the idea that exchange of one's sex is possible. It, like the storied Emperor, is starkly, nakedly false. Transgendered men do not become women, nor do transgendered women become men. All (including Bruce Jenner) become feminized men or masculinized women, counterfeits or impersonators of the sex with which they 'identify.' In that lies their problematic future.

When 'the tumult and shouting dies,' it proves not easy nor wise to live in a counterfeit sexual garb. The most thorough follow-up of sex-reassigned people – extending over thirty years and conducted in Sweden, where the culture is strongly supportive of the transgendered – documents their lifelong mental unrest. Ten to fifteen years after surgical reassignment, the suicide rate of those who had undergone sex-reassignment surgery rose to twenty times that of comparable peers.[22]

---

[21] Paul McHugh, 'Transgenderism: A Pathogenic Meme', *Public Discourse*, 10 June 2015, article at file:///C:/Users/Martin/Documents/EGGS%20PRT/Transgender/Transgenderism_%20A%20Pathogenic%20Meme%20_%20Public%20Discourse.html

[22] McHugh, 'Transgenderism: A Pathogenic Meme'.

As he sees it, the central issue that needs to be addressed in the case of transgender people is 'the assumption that one's sexual nature is misaligned with one's biological sex.' This assumption, he argues, has several different causes and the distinctions between them should determine how it should be managed and treated in the case of any particular individual.

> Based on the photographic evidence one might guess Bruce Jenner falls into the group of men who come to their disordered assumption through being sexually aroused by the image of themselves as women. He could have been treated for this misaligned arousal with psychotherapy and medication. Instead, he found his way to surgeons who worked him over as he wished. Others have already commented on his stereotypic caricature of women as decorative 'babes' ('I look forward to wearing nail polish until it chips off,' he said to Diane Sawyer) – a view that understandably infuriates feminists – and his odd sense that only feelings, not facts, matter here.
>
> For his sake, however, I do hope that he receives regular, attentive follow-up care, as his psychological serenity in the future is doubtful. Future men with similar feelings and intentions should be treated for those feelings rather than being encouraged to undergo bodily changes. Group therapies are now available for them.
>
> Most young boys and girls who come seeking sex-reassignment are utterly different from Jenner. They have no erotic interest driving their quest. Rather, they come with psychosocial issues – conflicts over the prospects, expectations, and roles that they sense are attached to their given sex – and presume that sex-reassignment will ease or resolve them.
>
> The grim fact is that most of these youngsters do not find therapists willing to assess and guide them in ways that permit them to work out their conflicts and correct their assumptions. Rather, they and their families find only 'gender counselors' who encourage them in their sexual misassumptions.
>
> There are several reasons for this absence of coherence in our mental health system. Important among them is the fact that both the state and federal governments are actively seeking to block any treatments that can be construed as challenging the assumptions and choices of transgendered youngsters. 'As part of our dedication to protecting America's youth, this administration supports efforts to ban the use of conversion therapy for minors,' said Valerie Jarrett,

a senior advisor to President Obama.

In two states, a doctor who would look into the psychological history of a transgendered boy or girl in search of a resolvable conflict could lose his or her license to practice medicine. By contrast, such a physician would not be penalized if he or she started such a patient on hormones that would block puberty and might stunt growth.

What is needed now is public clamor for coherent science – biological and therapeutic science – examining the real effects of these efforts to 'support' transgendering. Although much is made of a rare 'intersex' individual, no evidence supports the claim that people such as Bruce Jenner have a biological source for their transgender assumptions. Plenty of evidence demonstrates that with him and most others, transgendering is a psychological rather than a biological matter.

In fact, gender dysphoria – the official psychiatric term for feeling oneself to be of the opposite sex – belongs in the family of similarly disordered assumptions about the body, such as anorexia nervosa and body dysmorphic disorder. Its treatment should not be directed at the body as with surgery and hormones any more than one treats obesity-fearing anorexic patients with liposuction. The treatment should strive to correct the false, problematic nature of the assumption and to resolve the psychosocial conflicts provoking it. With youngsters, this is best done in family therapy.

The larger issue is the meme itself. The idea that one's sex is fluid and a matter open to choice runs unquestioned through our culture and is reflected everywhere in the media, the theater, the classroom, and in many medical clinics. It has taken on cult-like features: its own special lingo, internet chat rooms providing slick answers to new recruits, and clubs for easy access to dresses and styles supporting the sex change. It is doing much damage to families, adolescents, and children and should be confronted as an opinion without biological foundation wherever it emerges.[23]

3.5. Transgender and the Biblical witness

As we have seen, the basic belief underlying the arguments that are put forward for the acceptance of chosen identity of transgender people is the belief that there can be a person whose true, God given, sexual

---

[23] McHugh, 'Transgenderism: A Pathogenic Meme'.

identity is male or female, but who has a body of the opposite sex. This belief is incompatible with the creation narratives in Genesis 1 and 2.

These narratives teach that human beings are made in God's image and likeness (Genesis 1:26-27) as beings who have material bodies made from 'the dust of the ground' (Genesis 2:7). According to Genesis it is the entire person, body and soul together, who is created by God. In the words of Gerhard von Rad in his commentary on Genesis: 'one will do well to split the physical from the spiritual as little as possible: the whole man is created in God's image.'[24] This means, as Martin Luther puts it in his *Small Catechism,* that accepting the teaching of Genesis means believing 'that God has created me and all that exists; that he has given me and still sustains my body and soul, all my limbs and senses, my reason and all the faculties of my mind.'[25]

Furthermore these narratives (and the Bible as a whole) also teach that human beings are created by God as male and female with a vocation to 'be fruitful and multiply' (Genesis 1:28) that is to be fulfilled in the context of the one flesh sexual union of marriage (Genesis 2:24, 4:1). Human beings fulfil this vocation according to the ways that their bodies have been created, with those with male bodies fulfilling it as fathers and those with female bodies fulfilling it as mothers.

What all this means is that it makes no theological sense in the light of the Genesis creation narratives to separate self and body so that there can be a female self and a male body, or to claim that those with male bodies can claim to be mothers or vice versa.

In addition, Luther's reminder that God has not just created the world in general, but our particular form of existence means that we have to acknowledge that there are limits to the extent to which, to quote Tanis, we are 'called to be artisans of our own lives and bodies.' The starting point for our shaping of our lives has to be the grateful recognition that we have been created by God as part of a dimorphic sexual structure within which human beings exist as embodied creatures who are determined by their biology as either male or female. In the words of O'Donovan:

> The dimorphic structure, with its orientation towards permanent heterosexual union, is the generically given foundation for our individual sexual vocations. The first obligation of every human

---

24 Gerhard von Rad, *Genesis* (London: SCM, 1972), p 58.

25 Luther, *Small Catechism,* text in Mark Noll, *Confessions and Catechisms of the Reformation* (Vancouver: Regent College Publishing, 2004), p 68.

being is to hail that created givenness as a created good and to thank God for it, even though he or she may then have to acknowledge that for him or her in particular this created good has taken on the aspect of a problem.[26]

The appeals that are made to God's creation of 'in-between' things or to the androgynous nature of the first human being in Genesis 2 are unconvincing. The examples that are given of in-between things, such as dawn, dusk or the sea shore, are actually examples of names for times or places at the edge of things (dawn or dusk at the beginning or end of the day, and the sea shore at the end of the land) they do not describe mixed things. Furthermore in the Bible there are no examples of mixed human beings. Human beings are exclusively either male or female.

This raises the question of where intersex people fit into the biblical picture. Is it not the case, it is asked, that they have to be seen as examples of in between people who have been created by God in a way that falls outside the normal division between male and female? This is the argument put forward, as we have seen, by Tanis and also in more detail by the American writer Megan De Franza in her book *Sex Difference in Christian Theology*.[27]

However, the argument that people with an intersex condition constitute a third sex alongside being male or female fails to stand up to a careful scrutiny of the nature of intersex conditions. Such a scrutiny still continues to uphold the Genesis picture of the existence of only two sexes. This is a point made very clearly by Alastair Roberts in a podcast responding to De Franza' book. In it he asks 'Must the recognition of intersex persons involve denial that humanity is sexually dimorphic, or present resistance to that fact?' His response is as follows:

> Few of us would consider denying that humanity is a bipedal species on account of children born without a leg and persons who have legs amputated later in life. Medical science has acquainted us with processes of sex differentiation in the womb and, from its vantage point, most intersex conditions would seem to be appropriately classified as 'disorders of sex development'. The natural purposes of the sex organs and the human reproductive system – of which male and female both possess a half – are not just dark and unknown mysteries to us and it would seem strange not to be able to speak of natural processes going awry in certain cases.

---

26 O'Donovan, *Transsexualism: Issues and Argument*, pp 19-20.

27 Megan De Franza, *Sex Difference in Christian Theology* (Grand Rapids: Eerdmans, 2015).

It seems clear to me, as it generally seems to be to medical science, that human bodies are structured to be sexually reproductive – to be male and female – and humanity is a sexually dimorphic species. There is clearly considerable natural variation consistent with humanity's dimorphic form, but there is an obvious difference in principle between variation and defect, even if not always clear in the most marginal cases in practice, where, for instance, function may be retained in an abnormal or impaired form (abnormal forms are not necessarily defective forms, although they frequently are). Sexual organs with intersex conditions are typically characterized by defect – usually manifested in infertility, for instance – and can't adequately perform certain functions that sexual organs are supposed to perform.

This being the case, he says:

Intersex bodies and bodies with intersex conditions are not evidence of further sexes in addition to male and female, even though particular types of intersex conditions may possess distinct and identifiable characteristics. The sexual organs of intersex persons are not ordered to some different sexual end of their own, but are abnormally and/or defectively lacking in the typical functional male or female form, imperfectly related to the ends of male and female sexual organs. Their abnormality is usually connected with evidence that the ordinary processes of sexual differentiation have gone awry in some recognizable manner. That they are generally considered defective doesn't arise from the rarity of such conditions, but from the fact that they can't effectively do what sexual organs are supposed to be able to do. They are disordered male or female bodies, or bodies that are neither male nor female. At the very least, to claim that they are a further sex would seem to require some far-reaching re-evaluation of how we determine bodily organs to be functional or not.

There may be some sort of an empirical spectrum between male and female, albeit one overwhelmingly populated at the poles. However, the existence of such an empirical spectrum is not proof against sexual dimorphism, because there remain only two functional forms of sex around which specific human beings are clustered. All intermediate forms are departures from these, without an integral purpose of their own.[28]

---

[28] Alastair Roberts, Podcast, Intersex, *Mere Fidelity,* 25 August, 2015, text at https://alastairadversaria.com/2015/08/25/podcast-intersex/

Looking at intersex conditions in this light means saying, as O'Donovan does, that what we have in the case of the bodies of people with such conditions is 'an ambiguity which has arisen by a malfunction in a dimorphic human sexual pattern.'[29] As Roberts goes on to say, acknowledging the existence of such a malfunction, acknowledging that there is a defect of some sort, then challenges us to think about the specific 'possibilities of vocation' for people who have such a defect.[30] It is the start rather than the end of a conversation. However, acknowledging that a malfunction has occurred, rather than claiming the existence of a third sex, is at least the right place to start the conversation.

The idea that Genesis 2 describes an originally sexually undifferentiated earth creature is not supported by the text. As Richard Davidson explains

> According to 2:7-8, 15-16, what God creates before woman is called *ha adam*, 'the man,' better translated as 'the human.' After the creation of woman, this creature is denoted by the same term (vv 22-23). Nothing has changed in the makeup of 'the human' during his sleep except the loss of a rib. There is no hint in the text of an originally bisexual or sexually undifferentiated being split into two different sexes. The androgynous interpretation suggests that human beings are not intrinsically sexual, a view which contradicts the anthropology of Gen 1-2. According to the biblical text *ha adam*, 'the human' formed before woman was not originally androgynous but was 'created in anticipation of the future.' He was created with those sexual drives towards union with his counterpart. This becomes apparent in the first human's encounter with the animals, which dramatically pointed up his need of 'a helper as his partner' (vv.18-20). Such a need is satisfied when he is introduced to woman and he fully realizes his sexuality vis-à-vis his sexual complement.[31]

What is more, even if it was the case that *ha adam* was originally androgynous there is nothing in Genesis 2 or elsewhere in the Bible to suggest that this androgyny is an original wholeness to which subsequent human beings might want to return. On the contrary, in Genesis 1 and 2 the division of humanity into male and female is the culmination of God's good act of creation and so nowhere is it

---

29 O'Donovan, *Transsexualism: Issues and Argument*, p 8.
30 Roberts Podcast, Intersex.
31 Richard Davidson, *Flame of Yahweh – Sexuality in the Old Testament* (Peabody: Hendrickson, 2007), pp 20-21.

suggested that androgyny is a state to which human beings could or should want to return.[32]

In the Bible eunuchs do not form an exception to the binary distinction between men and women. This is because the term eunuch refers to men who for some reason lack sexual capacity (and are therefore incapable of entering into marriage). Thus the standard dictionary of New Testament Greek offers three possibilities for the word *eunouchos*. The first is 'a castrated male person' (Matthew 19:12, Esther 2:14, Acts 8:27ff). The second is 'a human male who, without a physical operation, is by nature incapable of begetting children' (Wisdom 3:14, Matthew 19:12) and the third is 'a human male who abstains from marriage without being impotent, a celibate' (Matthew 19:12).[33]

This being the case, the welcome extended to eunuchs in Isaiah 56:1-5, Matthew 19:10-12 and Acts 8:26-40 cannot be understood as biblical support for those who are transgendered because the eunuchs referred to in the Bible were not transgendered. They were, as we have said, men who lacked sexual capacity. It is true that this made them 'gender variant' in the sense of being outside the norm for men of their culture, but this does not mean they were transgender.

It is true that the Bible extends a welcome to eunuchs in spite of their gender variance, but it still sees them as having their original

---

[32] Jesus' saying about there being no marriage in heaven (Matthew 22:30) does not mean that we shall be androgynous in the world to come. All it is saying is that there will be no marriage as we know it in heaven.

As Glynn Harrison notes in his book, *A better story* (IVP 2016) the Bible as a whole teaches that earthly marriage will be transcended by that to which it points, namely the marriage between Christ and his Church. However, this does not mean that we will not still be male and female. To deny this would involve what John Calvin calls the 'monstrous error' of 'those who imagine that the soul, instead of resuming the body with which it is now clothed, will obtain a new and different body' (*Institutes* Bk.III: 25:7).

We are creatures who are created by God in two sexes and, as St. Augustine says, at the resurrection 'he who established the two sexes will restore them both' (*City of God* XXII:18). That is why at Jesus' own resurrection and in all the other acts of resurrection in the Bible which prefigure it or reflect it people come back to bodily life in their original sex (think the widow's son at Zarephath, Jairus' daughter, the widow's son at Nain, Lazarus, Dorcas etc.). The resurrection is the completion not the abrogation of creation.

[33] W. Arndt, F. W Danker, F. Wilbur Gingrich and Walter Bauer, *A Greek-English Lexicon of the New Testament and Other Early Christian Literature* (Chicago: University of Chicago Press, 2000), p 409.

created identity as male. They are not seen as exceptions to the universal binary division between male and female.

It is also true that the New Testament uses gender variant language when describing the Church. Women are indeed called brothers (Romans 14:10, 1 Corinthians 6:5-6). All Christians, regardless of sex, constitute the bride of Christ (Ephesians 5:25-27). All Christians, including female Christians, are parts of the body of the male Christ (Ephesians 5:30). However two things need to be noted in relation to this language. First, this language is metaphorical and as such is not intended to describe the human sexual identity of the people concerned. Secondly, in line with this fact the New Testament continues to divide the Church into men and women (as in the advice about Christian conduct contained in passages such as Ephesians 5:22-33, 1 Timothy 2:8-15 and 1 Peter 3:1-7). A clear division between those who are male and those who are female continues to be maintained.

The same is true in regard to Galatians 3:28. This verse needs to be read in the context of the whole of Galatians 3:23-29 which runs as follows:

> Now before faith came, we were confined under the law, kept under restraint until faith should be revealed. So that the law was our custodian until Christ came, that we might be justified by faith. But now that faith has come, we are no longer under a custodian; for in Christ Jesus you are all sons of God, through faith. For as many of you as were baptized into Christ have put on Christ. *There is neither Jew nor Greek, there is neither slave nor free, there is neither male nor female; for you are all one in Christ Jesus.* And if you are Christ's, then you are Abraham's offspring, heirs according to promise.

Seen in this wider context it is clear that verse 28 (in italics) is not about sexual identity but about spiritual identity. What these verses are saying is that anyone who has faith in Jesus Christ and is baptised (regardless of their race, social standing or sex) is an inheritor of the promise of divine blessing made to Abraham and as such part of the family of God. So men and women do not cease to be men and women, but this distinction does not count in relation to their being heirs of the promise to Abraham.

It follows that neither the gender variant language used to refer to the Church nor Galatians 3:28 have any relevance to the transgender issue.

What is said in the Bible about the eschatological transformation of creation, about our participation in Christ's death and resurrection and about people receiving a new name does not provide support for the idea that people can have a sexual identity that is at variance with their bodies.

As Richard Bauckham explains in his study of the theology of the Book of Revelation, the promise of a 'new heaven and a new earth' in Revelation 21:1, based on the prophecies in Isaiah 65:17 and 66:22, is not a promise of the replacement of the existing creation with an entirely new one. Rather, it is a promise that God will give the present creation 'a quite new form of existence, taken beyond all threat of evil and destruction, indwelt by his own glory, participating in his own eternity.'[34] This is also what St. Paul means in Romans 8:21 when he says that 'creation itself will be set free from its bondage to decay and obtain the glorious liberty of the children of God.'

The way in which God's people participate in this eschatological renewal of creation is through participating in the death and resurrection of Christ. We can see this in St. Paul's words in Romans 6:5-11:

> For if we have been united with him in a death like his, we shall certainly be united with him in a resurrection like his. We know that our old self was crucified with him so that the sinful body might be destroyed, and we might no longer be enslaved to sin. For he who has died is freed from sin. But if we have died with Christ, we believe that we shall also live with him. For we know that Christ being raised from the dead will never die again; death no longer has dominion over him. The death he died he died to sin, once for all, but the life he lives he lives to God. So you also must consider yourselves dead to sin and alive to God in Christ Jesus.

In 1 Corinthians 15:44 St. Paul refers to the mode of existence that God's people will share in the resurrection as a 'spiritual body.' However, this does not mean that our present physical bodies will be replaced by a new non material form of existence. As Tom Wright states in his commentary on 1 Corinthians, that is 'exactly what he is *not* saying.' Instead, the contrast St. Paul is making:

> ...is between a body animated by one type of life and a body animated by another type. The difference between them is found, if you like, on what the two bodies run on. The present body is animated by the normal life which all humans share. The word Paul uses for this often means 'soul'; he means it in the sense of the

---

[34] Richard Bauckham, *The Theology of the Book of Revelation* (Cambridge: CUP, 1993), p 49.

ordinary life-force on which we all depend in this present body, the ordinary energy that keeps us breathing and our blood circulating. But the body that we shall be given in the resurrection is to be animated by God's own spirit. This is what Paul says in a simpler passage, Romans 8:10-11: the spirit of Jesus the Messiah dwells within you at the moment, and God will give life to your mortal bodies through this spirit who lives inside you.'[35]

What all this means is that our physical bodies are an eternal part of our existence. In the life of the world to come we shall have physical bodies just as we have now, only animated by the Spirit and thereby made imperishable and immortal (1 Corinthians 15:52-54). This means that if because of our form of embodiment we are men in this life we shall be men in the world to come and if we are women we shall be women in the world to come. We can see the truth of this in the case of Jesus, who is in his humanity the 'first fruits' (1 Corinthians 15:23) of the new form of human existence created by his death and resurrection. In his humanity Jesus was a male human being with a male body and it was this same body that was resurrected (Luke 24:36-42), which subsequently ascended into heaven and which will return to earth when Jesus comes in glory (Acts 1:9-11).

The fact that our bodies will be part of our existence for all eternity once again reinforces the basic point that our sexed bodies are an integral part of who we are. God does not reject our bodies, but gives them an immortal existence. Therefore we are not free to reject our bodies by rejecting the sexual identity that they give us.

If we turn to those passages in the Bible where people are given new names we find that this new name reflects a change in someone's identity. Thus Jacob becomes Israel, 'he who strives with God,' after he wrestled all night with God at the ford over the Jabbok (Genesis 32:22-32). Thus Simon became Peter, 'the rock,' because as the leader of the Apostles he was going to be foundation stone on which God would build his Church (Matthew 16:18). However nowhere in the Bible do we find a new name given to someone to express their sense of their own sexual identity at variance with that of their body.

This means that in the liturgy we looked at in chapter 1 of this report it was illegitimate to use the examples of the re-naming of Abraham, Sarah, Jacob, Peter and Paul as biblical precedent for giving Mary the male name Asher. In the case of the biblical examples there is a real change of identity

---

35   Tom Wright, *Paul for Everyone - 1 Corinthians* (London: SPCK, 2003), p 221.

reflected in the change of name, but in the case of Asher the new name does not reflect a real change of identity because as someone with a female embodiment, biblically speaking Asher is still a woman.

The prohibition of cross-dressing in Deuteronomy 22:5 can be seen as relevant to the current debate about transgender issues. This is because, as Peter Harland writes in his study of this verse, the rationale behind this provision is that:

> To dress after the manner of the opposite sex was to infringe the natural order of creation which divided humanity into male and female. That distinction was fundamental to human existence and could not be blurred in any way, hence the rule of Dt 22:5.[36]

To quote Davidson, because this prohibition is grounded in the order of creation; 'it may be concluded that the intent was for this legislation to be permanent (transtemporal) and universal (transcultural) in its application.'[37]

That this is the case can be seen by the teaching of St. Paul in 1 Corinthians 11:2-16 in which he tells the Christians in Corinth 'that in worship men should follow the dress and hair codes which proclaim them to be male and women the codes which proclaim them to be female.'[38] As Wright goes on to explain, the reason for this is because 'God's creation needs humans to be fully, gloriously and truly human, which means fully and truly male and female.'[39] The nature of these codes in any particular cultural setting can be a matter for legitimate debate, but what is indisputable is the biblical principle that men are meant to express their God given maleness and women their God given femaleness. From a biblical standpoint forms of behaviour that go against this principle are problematic.

3.6. Jesus and transgender

It is true that according to both Matthew 2:18-25 and Luke 1:26-37 Jesus was born from the Virgin Mary without a human father. However, the claim that this means that he must have been intersex, with female chromosomes but a male body, rests on the assumption that what we

---

36 P.J. Harland 'Menswear and Womenswear: A Study of Deuteronomy 22:5,' *Expository Times*, 110, No.3,1988, p 76.
37 Davidson, *Flame of Yahweh*, p 172.
38 Wright, *Paul for Everyone – 1 Corinthians*, p 142.
39 Wright, *Paul for Everyone – 1 Corinthians*, p 143.

are dealing with in these stories is an example of natural parthenogenesis. However, both stories make clear that what they are in fact talking about is not a natural event, however rare, but the miraculous activity of God through his Spirit.

We cannot predict in advance what the result of such divine activity will be. All we can do is look at the evidence for what God did do and what the New Testament tells us unequivocally is that Jesus was in his humanity a male human being. All the New Testament accounts of Jesus without exception testify to this. Accordingly, the argument that Jesus was intersex can only be maintained in the face of the available evidence and should therefore be discarded.

It is also true that Jesus was 'queer' in the sense that he went against the conventional expectations of his society, but there is no evidence that this 'queerness' extended to his challenging the idea that those with male bodies are men and those with female bodies are women. This might be challenged as an argument from silence. What evidence do we have that Jesus did not accept this idea? However, the counter to this is the fact that when Jesus did challenge the conventional Jewish ideas of his day there are records of it in the gospel. The fact that there are no records in the gospels that Jesus challenged the idea that people's bodies define their sex therefore indicates that he did not do so.

It is further true that Jesus remained the same person while undergoing a process of transition that took him through the incarnation and his earthly ministry to death, resurrection and ascension. It is also true that he combined humanity and divinity and death and resurrection. However, the fact that Jesus went through a process of transition ordained by God for the sake of our salvation does not mean that it is right for others to go through a process of transition in which they seek to deny the God given sexual identity indicated by their biology. Likewise the fact that Jesus was both human and divine and held together in himself both death and resurrection does not mean that transgender people combine being both male and female. As noted above, from a biblical perspective they are of one sex even if they desire to be of another.

3.7.   Job's Comforters?

According to the book of Job, God declares that the fault of Job's comforters lies in the fact they 'have not spoken of me what is right' (Job 32:7). In specific terms, they have claimed that God is punishing

Job for his sins and requires that Job should repent, whereas in fact neither is true.

This means that for the claim that those who are critical of gender transition are like Job's comforters to be justified, the critics have to be speaking untruthfully about God. In specific terms this would mean that they are wrong in their claim that God has created people to live according to the sex of their bodies. However, the evidence that we have looked at in this chapter indicates that this claim is not wrong. It follows that those who are critical of gender transition are not acting as Job's comforters, but as those who are truthfully describing how God has created human beings and desires that they should live.

It is certainly true that all in the church need to offer people afflicted with gender dysphoria love, acceptance and support, and should affirm the virtuous aspects of the lives of transgender people. However, it does not follow that they should therefore affirm gender transition. As we have seen in this chapter, the idea of gender transition is philosophically and theologically problematic and it is far from clear that going through gender transition leads to the relief of mental suffering that those with gender dysphoria seek to achieve.

This chapter has looked critically at the arguments put forward in support of gender transition and found them wanting. The next chapter will go on to sketch out an alternative Christian theological framework for approaching the issue of gender transition and for giving pastoral care for people with gender dysphoria.

4. A Christian approach to the issue of gender transition

4.1. God's creation of humanity

When thinking about the issue of gender transition from a Christian perspective the starting point has to be what is said about God's creation of humanity in the creation narratives in Genesis 1 and 2. This is because although each individual human being is individually created by God (Job 10:8, Psalm 119:73, 139:13) they are made according to the pattern laid down in Genesis 1 and 2. There is no suggestion anywhere in the Bible that God creates people in a way that deviates from that pattern.

If we ask what that pattern is then the answer, as we saw in the last chapter, is that human beings are made as embodied creatures and as sexual creatures. They are creatures with bodies and these bodies are either male or female with the difference between them corresponding to the different role that men and women play in the act of sexual reproduction. Men, that is to say, are made with an embodiment that allows them to be fathers and women are made with an embodiment that allows them to be mothers. Obviously because of circumstance, accident, disease, or a calling to celibacy, not all men will be fathers, and not all women will be mothers, but they are created with an orientation to this goal in accordance with God's command to his human creatures to 'be fruitful and multiply' (Genesis 1:28).

This biblical view of how God created human beings to be is supported by observation of what we learn from observing the way in which human beings exist. In the words of Christopher Tollefsen when we look at human beings we find that:

> Our identity as animal organisms is the foundation of our existence as selves. But fundamental to our existence as this animal is our sex. We are male or female organisms in virtue of having a root capacity for reproductive function, even when that capacity is immature or damaged. In human beings, as well as in many other organisms, that function is one to be performed jointly with another human being; unlike the digestive function, no individual human being suffices for its performance.

> Accordingly, reproductive function in human beings is distributed across the two sexes, which are identified by their having the root

capacity for one or the other of the two general structural and behavioral patterns involved in human reproduction. In male humans, this capacity is constituted by the structures necessary for the production of male gametes and the performance of the male sex act, insemination. In females, the capacity is constituted by the structures necessary for the production of oocytes and the performance of the female sex act, the reception of semen in a manner disposed to conception.[1]

What the Bible tells us that the observation of human nature cannot is that the sexual distinction of human beings into male and female by reason of their bodies is something that exists not only in this world, but also in the world to come. As we noted in the previous chapter, the biblical teaching about the resurrection of the body teaches us that we will live in the world to come in bodies animated by the Spirit and therefore immortal, but still fundamentally the same bodies that we possess in this world. This means that men will live for ever as men and women will live for ever as women. Who we are according to the sexual differentiation of our bodies is thus who we shall be forever.

4.2. Why the existence of sexual differentiation between men and women is very good.

According to Genesis 1:31 God's creation of human beings as men and women with sexually differentiated bodies is something that is 'very good.' There are a number of reasons why this is the case.

First, God's creation of human beings as men and women is good because it allows the human race to continue. Without bodily sexual differentiation reproduction could not happen and so the human race would cease to exist.

Secondly, God's creation of human beings as men and women is good because it allows for the kind of sexual delight and pleasure that is described for us, for example, in the Song of Solomon. It is the way that human beings are created to allow for sexual reproduction that also makes possible the pleasure of sexual intercourse (something which is true even if that intercourse takes place between two people of the same sex).

---

[1] Christopher Tollefsen, 'Sex Identity,' *Public Discourse*, 12 July 2015, text at file:///C:/Users/Martin/Documents/EGGS%20PRT/Transgender/Sex%20Identity%20%20Public%20Discourse.htm

Thirdly, God's creation of human beings as men and women who have sexual desire for each other, who marry, and who engage in sexual reproduction is good because it points us towards God in a number of ways:

- The fruitful nature of sex and sexual relationships, both in producing offspring and (when well ordered) in providing the basis for strong families and strong communities, points us to the fruitful nature of the love that exists within the Triune life of God himself, a love that is fruitful in calling the universe into being and in creating a family of human beings to be in relationship with God and to share with him in his rule over creation. As God's image bearers human beings are called to 'be fruitful and multiply' (Genesis 1:28) because in so doing they bear witness to the fruitful nature of God's love.

- Our experience of sexual desire points us towards the passionate nature of God's love for us. In the words of Glynn Harrison '...our sexual attractions and desires – our embodied experience – shows us the passionate nature of God's love. We can learn about it in our heads, but the experience of our bodies brings it home to our hearts.' [2]

- The fact that our sexual desires, like all our other earthly desires, are never fully satisfied points us to the truth that it is only in the relationship with God in the world to come that the saving work of Jesus Christ has made possible that we shall find satisfaction for the deepest desires of our hearts. To quote the well-known words of St. Augustine, what the unfulfilled nature of our sexual desires shows us is that 'Thou hast formed us for Thyself, and our hearts are restless till they find rest in thee.' [3]

- Sexual faithfulness within marriage points us to the faithful nature of God's love for us. To quote Harrison again:

In the Bible sex is inextricably bound up bound up with the covenant of marriage, presented to us as a permanent, 'for-better-for-worse,' lifelong commitment of faithfulness. Similarly, God's love for us is also presented as faithful, covenantal and permanent: it doesn't waver; he doesn't do one-night stands; he doesn't grow tired of us; he doesn't 'fall in love' with somebody else. Marriage is

---

2   Glynn Harrison, *A Better Story* (London: IVP, 2016), Kindle edition, Loc. 2026.
3   St Augustine, *Confessions* Bk 1:1, in *The Nicene and Post Nicene Fathers*, First Series, Vol 1, (Edinburgh and Grand Rapids, T&T Clark/Eerdmans, 1994), p 45.

an icon of God's faithfulness. And this great biblical institution puts this truth on display for all the world to see.[4]

- Furthermore, as Harrison says, it is not only sexual faithfulness within marriage but sexual abstinence outside it that bears witness to God's faithfulness:

> ...single Christians who abstain from sex *outside* the marriage bond bear witness to the faithful nature of God's love with the same authority as those who have sex *inside* the marriage bond. Both paint pictures of God's faithfulness, but in different ways...both single and married people who abstain from sex outside the marriage bond point to the same thing. They both 'deploy' their sexuality in ways that serve as a sign of the kingdom and the faithful character of God's passion. In refusing to have sex outside marriage, the single person witnesses to the unbreakable link between passion and faithfulness. And in refusing to commit adultery, the married person bears witness to the same truth.[5]

4.3. Rejection of the goodness of sexual differentiation

For the reasons just given, the sexual differentiation of humanity into men and women is something that we should embrace as good. However, there are a small but increasing number of people who reject the idea that the division of humanity into men and women is a good. They would argue that we need to move beyond what they call the 'gender binary' and instead accept the existence of multiple forms of human identity beyond simply being men and women. Only in this way will we bring to an end what they see as an oppressive gender hierarchy in which men are seen as superior to women and those who fit into the conventional categories of male and female are seen as superior to those who do not.[6]

In line with this approach there are now a variety of non-binary gender descriptions which have been developed by those who do not see themselves as accurately described as either men or women.

For example, the online Non-binary Gender Wiki explains that:

Those with non-binary genders can feel that they:

---

4   Harrison, *A Better Story.* Loc. 2026-36.
5   Harrison, *A Better Story.* Loc. 2046.
6   See Ken N Wickham, *The Other Genders: Androgyne, Genderqueer, Non-Binary Gender Variant* (Create Space, 2011).

- Have an androgynous (both masculine and feminine) gender identity, such as androgyne.

- Have an identity between male and female, such as intergender.

- Have a neutral or unrecognized gender identity, such as agender, neutrois, or most xenogenders.

- Have multiple gender identities, such as bigender or pangender.

- Have a gender identity which varies over time, known as genderfluid.

- Have a weak or partial connection to a gender identity, known as demigender.

- Are intersex and identify as intersex, known as amalgagender

- Have a culturally specific gender identity which exists only within their or their ancestor's culture.[7]

In line with the idea of a variety of genders the idea has also developed that there should be a variety of pronouns available to refer to people who do not view themselves as either male or female. Thus it has been suggested by a number of American universities such as Harvard, the University of Vermont, the University of Wisconsin-Milwaukee and the American University, Washington DC, that new pronouns such as ze, hir, hirs, zir, xe, xem or xyr should be used in order to be welcoming and inclusive to transgender students who do not wish to identify as either male or female.[8]

As part of this movement towards challenging the gender binary there are now Christian theologians who argue on theological grounds that we need to move beyond the traditional Christian division of humanity into male and female (and, indeed, beyond any idea of gender at all).

For example, Susannah Cornwall argues that as Christians we may need to be willing to give up our gender identity in order to discover what it means to be truly human:

> We speak about and interact with God as gendered beings. But God Godself is not gendered in the way that humans are, so the part of

7   http://gender.wikia.com/wiki/Non-binary.
8   See Caroline Moynihan, 'Pronouns and the march of gender diversity,' *Mercator Net*, 15 January 2016 https://www.mercatornet.com/conjugality/view/pronouns-and-the-march-of-gender-diversity/17461.

us that is – to borrow Grace Jantzen's phrase – becoming divine is not necessarily a part that needs to maintain gender as a central or critical aspect of selfhood. We reflect the image of an indubitably genderless God, as well as all the gendered quasi-gods of our own creation. As humans living in human societies it may still be appropriate to live out 'limited' human identities such as those grounded in binary gender; what is crucial is that it is accepted that this is a finite and penultimate aspect of being human. In order to know what it is to be *truly* human we may eventually have to let go of something that for many people seems the very essence of our humanity, our existence as gendered beings.[9]

She goes on to argue that it is in fact idolatrous to cling to one particular model of human gender (by which she means the division of humanity into male and female):

To cling to a particular model of human gender because it is thought to be central to human status as being in the image of God is not only unhelpful – as Morland implies – but also idolatrous. For humans cling solely to what they already believe to be true of God can only limit a fuller understanding of what it is actually possible to know of God ... the 'kenotic hymn' of Phil.2.5-11 counsels that humans are to emulate Jesus, who did not consider equality with God something to be grasped; but to exploit, to cling, or to grasp at equality with God is exactly what is happening when humans decide that a single ... reading of gender tells the whole story of God.[10]

For another example, Elizabeth Stuart argues in her essay 'The Priest at the Altar: The Eucharistic Erasure of Sex' that the priest celebrating the Eucharist represents a Church in which the distinction between men and women has been abolished through baptism:

The priest leads and represents the Church before the throne of God. Incorporation into this body through baptism involves the decentralizing of all defining classifications as the ancient baptismal formula cited by St Paul in Galatians 3.28 makes clear. In Christ there is no male or female. The ancient rite of blessing of the baptismal waters at the Easter Vigil speaks of the font as a womb through which humans are 'born again as new creatures ... a heavenly offspring ... that all who are distinguished either by sex in body or age in time, may be brought forth to the same infancy by

9   Susannah Cornwall, 'Apophasis and Ambiguity' in Marcella Althaus Reid and Lisa Isherwood (eds.), *Trans/Formations* (London: SCM, 2009), p 28.
10   Cornwall, 'Apophasis and Ambiguity', pp 31-32.

grace, their mother.' Into the font are plunged sex and age and what emerges is a new creation, the product of the resurrection. It is this new creation which the priest represents before God, a sexless humanity. This is humanity whose identity is erased by the very excess of it. No one is excluded and the act of inclusion obliterates identity which is always predicated upon exclusion.[11]

As we have seen, what we learn from the twin books of nature and Scripture is that God has created humanity as a sexually dimorphic species and that the sexual distinction between men and women is something that is very good, and that it is something that will endure for all eternity. The rejection of the gender binary by both secular thinkers and by theologians such as Cornwall and Stuart is a rejection of all this. Rather than seeing the distinction between men and women as something to be celebrated as a good gift from God, it sees this distinction as something which has to be overcome, or, as Stuart sees it, something that has already been overcome.

From the standpoint of orthodox Christian theology, such a rejection of God's goodness has to be seen as a form of the primal sin of eating the fruit of the tree of the knowledge of good and evil (Genesis 2:17). This is because it is an attempt by human beings to determine for themselves what is good and evil rather than being willing to submit to God's instruction about the matter. God has shown us what it means to be human. Rejecting the gender binary means deciding to go our own way instead.

Gender transition, by contrast, does not mean a rejection of sexually dimorphic character of humanity. The whole basis of gender transition lies in the belief of those who undergo transition that there *is* a real distinction between being male and being female. However, in their view they were placed on the wrong side of this distinction at birth, a mistake which they have corrected or are seeking to correct.

As we have seen in the work of Beardsley, Dowd and Tanis, transgender people believe profoundly that they have a sexed identity as either male or female. That is why they seek to live as members of their real sex. Unfortunately their body does not correspond to this reality so they seek to change their body so that it conforms more closely to who they really are.

---

[11] Elizabeth Stuart, 'The Priest at the Altar: The Eucharistic Erasure of Sex,' in Marcella Althaus Reid and Lisa Isherwood (eds.), *Trans/Formations* (London: SCM, 2009), p 132.

This means that they are not committing the same error as those who reject the gender binary. They not rejecting God's creation of humanity as male and female or seeking to overcome it. They want to live as men and women. However, what they are doing is rejecting the goodness of God's creation of humanity as male and female in their particular case. God has made them either male or female, but they reject this sexual identity in favour of claiming that they are the opposite sex.

They would, of course, not say that this is what they are doing. They would say that they accept their true God given sexual identities. The problem is that their bodies do not correspond to these identities.

However, by saying this they are rejecting the truth that sexual identity and embodiment cannot be separated. As we have seen, in order to argue for the truth of their desired sexual identity transgender people have to claim that they have a sexed self whose sex is different from the sex of the body with which they were born. As we have also seen, such a claim goes against the teaching of Scripture concerning the embodied nature of human sexual differentiation and is also incoherent because it is impossible to conceive of what it would mean for a disembodied self to have a sexual identity.

If we ask why transgender people therefore make this claim the answer is because they feel they are a member of the opposite sex. If we then ask why they feel this way the answer from a biblical perspective is that they feel this way because, like all the other descendants of Adam, they are sinners (Romans 5:12-21, Psalm 143:2, 1 Kings 8:46 Romans 3:10-23).

4.4. Gender Transition and sin.

In order to understand the link between the feelings of transgender people and sin we need to begin by looking at what the Bible has to say about how sin affects human beings.

Sin is the spiritual force or power that prevents human beings from living in the way God intends. How it does this is helpfully explained by Stanley Grenz in his book *Theology for the People of God*. He notes that according to Scripture sin infects our hearts, corrupts our affections and holds us in bondage.

> The authors of Scripture assert that the human predicament results from the corrupt *heart* (e.g. Rom. 7:18; Eph.2:3; Jer. 17:9). By this they mean that sin has found lodging within us – in the core of our personal being.

The Scriptures teach that sin affects a person's entire heart. It infects our personal 'control centre.' Paul describes this situation in vivid terms. He speaks of sin as causing our 'our foolish hearts' to be 'darkened' (Rom.1:21) and our minds to be 'corrupt' (1 Tim 6:5). Because of sin, the apostle declares, we cannot understand spiritual truths (1 Cor.12:14; 2 Cor.4:4), and our thinking has become 'futile' (Rom. 1:21). In fact, our mind is hostile to God (Rom. 8:7-8).

In infecting the human heart, sin has likewise corrupted our *affections*. Sinful human beings are 'enslaved by all kinds of passions and pleasures' (Titus 3:3). And because our deeds are evil we love darkness rather than light (John 3:19).

The New Testament asserts that the sin which now resides in the core of our being enslaves its prey. It is a power that rules our lives, for sinning gives evidence of our bondage to sin. Hence, Jesus declares, 'I tell you the truth, everyone who sins is a slave to sin' (John 8:24). And both Paul (Rom. 6:16-17, 20) and Peter (2 Peter 2:19) assert that we are slaves to whatever masters us.[12]

Because sin infects and controls our lives in this way we commit specific acts of sin. That is why St. Paul talks in Galatians 5:19-21 about 'the works of the flesh' which he lists as 'fornication, impurity, licentiousness, idolatry, sorcery, enmity, strife, jealousy, anger, selfishness, dissension, party spirit, drunkenness and the like.' These particular sinful forms of behaviour are the works performed by the 'flesh,' that is to say, human nature infected and controlled by sin.

The connection between sin and particular sins can be analysed in terms of the corruption of the mind, leading to wrong desire, and hence to the performance of wrong acts. If we take adultery as an example, we find that what takes place is that the mind of an adulterer, being corrupted by sin, wrongly believes that it would be a good thing to have sex with someone who is married to someone else. This leads to the desire to have such sex and this in turn then leads to the act of adultery itself. If we take theft as a second example, we find that the mind of a thief wrongly believes that it would be good to have something that belongs to someone else. This leads to the desire to have that thing and hence to the act of theft.

If we transfer this analysis to the issue of gender transition what we find is that a person suffering from gender dysphoria, because their

---

[12] Stanley Grenz, *Theology for the Community of God* (Carlisle: Paternoster press, 1994), pp 239-40.

mind is corrupted by sin, wrongly believes that they are a member of the opposite sex to that of their biology, this leads to the desire to live like that and hence to gender transition.[13]

Because human beings have the ability to know God's will, either through their acquaintance with the teaching of Scripture or through the revelation of God's will given through nature and conscience, they can experience a discrepancy between what sin is telling them to believe and do and what they learn about God's will from these sources. This leads to the kind of conflict recorded by St. Paul in Romans 7 in which someone knows that they ought to resist sin, but lacks the ability to do so. 'I do not do the good I want, but the evil I do not want is what I do' (Romans 7:18). In a similar fashion the stories told by transgender people often record a period of sometimes intense struggle in which they fight against their gender dysphoria, but eventually decide that they will only find peace if they come to accept and live out that which sin misleads them into believing is their true identity.

Of course, transgender people would not see themselves as being misled by sin, and this not how they describe their stories. But if they are being led to believe what is contrary to God's truth and to act upon it, then in terms of Christian theology this must be said to be the result of sin. It should be noted, however, that saying that gender dysphoria is a result of sin does not exclude the recognition of a range of secondary causes that may lead people to be susceptible to this condition.

In the case of alcoholism, for example, it is generally accepted that some people may have an inclination to abuse alcohol that is stronger than that of other people for a range of reasons that may include their biology, their psychological make up, the cultural and social influences they have experienced and the particular circumstances of their lives. However, acknowledging these influences does not preclude saying that their abuse of alcohol is a result of sin at work in their lives. Drunkenness is, as St. Paul says in Galatians 5:21, a work of 'the flesh.'

One could give a similar account of all and every other form of sin. There will always be secondary causes in a person's life which explain why they are susceptible to a particular form of sin and the same is true

---

[13] See, for example, the stories contained in Beardsley and O'Brien, (eds.), *This is my body – Hearing the theology of transgender Christians* (London: Darton, Longman and Todd, 2016) Part 2; in Helen Savage 'Changing sex?: transsexuality and Christian theology' Doctoral thesis, Durham University, 2006, Chapter 1, available at Durham E-Theses Online: http://etheses.dur.ac.uk/3364/ and in Leanne Tigert and Maren Tirabassi (eds.), *Transgendering Faith* (Cleveland: Pilgrim Press, 2004), Part 2.

of gender dysphoria and gender transition. People may be susceptible to gender dysphoria because of a variety of factors which may be biological, psychological, cultural, or familial in nature.[14] In the case of Walt Heyer, for example, his gender dysphoria and subsequent gender transition was linked to painful childhood experiences and to his suffering from an undiagnosed dissociative disorder.[15]

However, identifying such causes and saying that gender dysphoria and gender transition are a result of sin should be seen as complementary rather than alternative explanations of what is going on. To say that gender dysphoria and gender transition are a result of sin is to make a theological statement about how a particular set of feelings and a particular course of action go against the good that God wills for his human creatures. To say they are a result of, say, familial experiences, or psychological problems, or are exacerbated by cultural influences, is to describe the mechanisms by which sin wields power in someone's life.

Having said that it is legitimate, and indeed necessary, to describe gender dysphoria and gender transition as a result of sin in people's lives, it is also important to introduce two notes of caution.

The first is that it is not right to view those who suffer from gender dysphoria or who have undergone gender transition as being more sinful than anyone else. The teaching of Romans 3:23 is clear: 'all have sinned and fallen short of the glory of God.' Those who have not sinned in a particular way are still equally sinners who have no right to look down on others, but can only cry out in solidarity with them 'God, be merciful to me a sinner' (Luke 18:13).

The second is not to let a focus on sin lead to a neglect of the fact that the secondary causes of gender dysphoria still need to be addressed. Thus if someone suffers from gender dysphoria because of mental health issues then they will need to seek appropriate psychiatric help and if someone has unresolved issues from their past then these will need to be dealt with. The results of the fall are multi-faceted and each needs to be dealt with properly in their own way.

---

[14] For a discussion of possible causes see Yarhouse, *Understanding Gender Dysphoria* Ch 3.
[15] Walt Heyer, *A Transgender's Faith.*

4.5. Caring pastorally for those who have undergone gender transition.

4.5.1. Welcome

The starting point for providing pastoral care is the truth that transgender people are precious in the sight of God. They have been created by God and he cares about them like a widow cares for a lost coin, a shepherd cares for a lost sheep, or a father cares for a prodigal son (Luke 15:1-32). This being the case they should be welcomed by God's people. This is a point that is made by Vaughan Roberts who writes that Jesus:

> ...really did welcome everyone. He welcomed the misfits and the outcasts and the people who the self-righteous religious establishment dismissed and had nothing to do with. Jesus loved them and welcomed them.

> And when we move on to the book of Acts, we find, as far as we can tell, that the first Gentile (non-Jew) who became a Christian was an Ethiopian eunuch – someone who, in today's language, might be described as gender queer.

> So I hope very much that church families will follow the example of Jesus and show a warm, non-judging welcome to everyone. I was visiting one church, and saw someone arrive was very obviously transgender. I thought to myself 'How are they going to respond?' I wondered if they might turn away or show disgust, or just stare. But no – no one batted an eyelid. They greeted the individual with a smile and a kind word, just as they did for everyone else. And I thought. 'What a lovely thing that is.' Giving a warm welcome should be our first instinct.[16]

A church that is not prepared to extend a welcome to transgender people just as it would to anyone else is a church that has not yet grasped the unconditional nature of God's grace. The biblical message is that no one deserves to be welcomed by God and yet there is no category of people, no special group of sinners, who God does not welcome. If God has welcomed us in spite of our sin then we must welcome others too. As St. Paul writes in Romans 15:7 'Welcome one another therefore, as Christ has welcomed you, for the glory of God.'

---

[16] Vaughan Roberts, *Transgender* (The Good Book Company, 2016), p 67.

4.5.2. *Faith and Baptism*

•Because transgender people are precious in the eyes of God we also need to do what we can to make sure that they are rightly related to God through faith and baptism. This is because, to return to a point made earlier in this chapter, as descendants of Adam they are ensnared by sin and as such are by nature spiritually dead and under God's judgement.

St. Paul makes this point when he reminds the Christians in Ephesus:

> ... you were dead through the trespasses and sins in which you once walked, following the course of this world, following the prince of the power of the air, the spirit that is now at work in the sons of disobedience. Among these we all once lived in the passions of our flesh, following the desires of body and mind, and so we were by nature children of wrath, like the rest of mankind. (Ephesians 2:1-3)

Like the people to whom St. Paul is writing, transgender people are in triple bondage to the world, the flesh, and the devil, and this is not because they are transgender, but because they are human. The fact that they reject their God given sexual identity is not the reason they are spiritually dead and subject to judgement. Rather, this rejection is, as we have seen, an expression of the fact that as human beings they have a fallen nature. It is this fallen nature, which is the underlying cause of all the specific forms of sin in their life, which is the fundamental issue which needs dealing with in order for them to be set free from death and judgement.

This means that pastoral care for transgender people needs to tackle the issues that they are facing in a proper order. The first priority is not to address the issue of their sexual identity. The first priority is to address the fact that they have a fallen nature and so a fatal disease called sin affects every area of their life. Prioritising the issue of their sexual identity is like tackling someone's anger management issues while ignoring the fact that they need urgent treatment for a life threatening illness.

If that is the problem which transgender people (like all other people) face, then what is the solution? St. Paul goes on to tell us in the following verses of Ephesians 2:

> But God, who is rich in mercy, out of the great love with which he loved us, even when we were dead through our trespasses, made us alive together with Christ (by grace you have been saved), and raised us up with him, and made us sit with him in the heavenly places in

Christ Jesus, that in the coming ages he might show the immeasurable riches of his grace in kindness toward us in Christ Jesus. For by grace you have been saved through faith; and this is not your own doing, it is the gift of God – not because of works, lest any man should boast. For we are his workmanship, created in Christ Jesus for good works, which God prepared beforehand, that we should walk in them. (Ephesians 2:4-10)

In the words of John Stott in his commentary on Ephesians, what these verses tell us is that:

We were the objects of his wrath, *but God, out of the great love with which he loved us* had mercy upon us. We were dead, and dead men do not rise, *but God* made us alive with Christ. We were slaves, *but God* has raised us with Christ, and set us at his own right hand, in a position of honour and power. Thus God has taken action to reverse our condition in sin.[17]

What these verses also tell us is that God's gracious activity on our behalf becomes effective in our lives 'through faith.' As Martin Luther explains in his 1520 tract *The Freedom of a Christian*, this is because faith unites the soul with Christ as a bride is united with her bridegroom (Ephesians 5:31-32):

Christ is full of grace, life, and salvation. The soul is full of sins, death, and damnation. Now let faith come between them and sins, death, and damnation will be Christ's, while grace, life, and salvation will be the soul's; for if Christ is a bridegroom, he must take upon himself the things which are his bride's and bestow upon her the things that are his. If he gives her his body and very self, how shall he not give her all that is his? And if he takes the body of the bride; how shall he not take all that is hers?

Here we have a most pleasing vision not only of communion but of a blessed struggle and victory and salvation and redemption. Christ is God and man in one person. He has neither sinned nor died, and is not condemned, and he cannot sin, die, or be condemned; his righteousness, life, and salvation are unconquerable, eternal, omnipotent. By the wedding ring of faith he shares in the sins, death and pains of hell which are his bride's. As a matter of fact, he makes them his own and acts as if they were his own and as if he himself had sinned; he suffered, died, and descended into hell that

---

17 John Stott, *The Message of Ephesians* (Downers Grove & Leicester: Inter-Varsity Press, 1979), p 80.

he might overcome them all. Now since it was such a one who did all this, and death and hell could not swallow him up, these were necessarily swallowed up by him in a mighty duel; for his righteousness is greater than the sins of all men, his life stronger than death, his salvation more invincible than hell. Thus the believing soul by means of the pledge of his faith is free in Christ, its bridegroom, free from all sins, secure against death and hell and is endowed with the eternal righteousness, life and salvation of Christ its bridegroom.[18]

By grace, through faith, we are saved because Christ takes our sin and death upon himself and overcomes them through the power of his righteousness and everlasting life. It is for that reason we are delivered from judgement and raised from death to life.

Baptism also comes into the picture because baptism is the sacramental means through which faith is given expression and the benefits which it conveys are received. Christ died to put to death our old sinful nature and rose again to give us a new life in its place. In baptism God offers us what Christ has done for us and when we accept it in faith by being baptised then it becomes ours. This is why St. Paul declares in Romans 6:3-4 'Do you not know that all of us who have been baptized into Christ Jesus were baptized into his death? We were buried therefore with him by baptism into death, so that as Christ was raised from the dead by the glory of the Father, we too might walk in newness of life.'

In the case of those baptised as infants the link between faith and baptism still holds because those who bring them to baptism express faith on their behalf and they have the opportunity to ratify this faith for themselves when they become older.

What all this means is that pastoral care for those who are transgender (like pastoral care for anyone else) means helping them to come to a place where either they believe and are baptised, or to a place where they believe and re-affirm the promises made when they were baptised as an infant (in Church of England terms that means being confirmed).

4.5.3. The call to holiness of life

Because we have been given a new life through faith and baptism we are called to live accordingly.

---

[18] Martin Luther, *The Freedom of a Christian*, in Martin Luther, *Three Treatises* (Philadelphia: Fortress Press, 1978), pp.286-287.

Thus in Romans 6:11-14 St. Paul writes:

> So you also must consider yourselves dead to sin and alive to God in Christ Jesus. Let not sin therefore reign in your mortal bodies, to make you obey their passions. Do not yield your members to sin as instruments of wickedness, but yield yourselves to God as men who have been brought from death to life, and your members to God as instruments of righteousness. For sin will have no dominion over you, since you are not under law but under grace.

In similar fashion he writes in Ephesians 4:17-24:

> Now this I affirm and testify in the Lord, that you must no longer live as the Gentiles do, in the futility of their minds; they are darkened in their understanding, alienated from the life of God because of the ignorance that is in them, due to their hardness of heart; they have become callous and have given themselves up to licentiousness, greedy to practice every kind of uncleanness. You did not so learn Christ! – assuming that you have heard about him and were taught in him, as the truth is in Jesus. Put off your old nature which belongs to your former manner of life and is corrupt through deceitful lusts, and be renewed in the spirit of your minds, and put on the new nature, created after the likeness of God in true righteousness and holiness.

We are not left to our own resources to live in this way. As those who believe and are baptised we have the gift of the Holy Spirit (Acts 2:38) who is given to us to enable us to begin to become the people God has created and re-created us to be. However, the Spirit's work in our life is not automatic. We have a choice about whether we will receive the new life that the Spirit has to give or whether we will continue to live according to the pattern of our old nature ('the flesh'). St. Paul highlights this choice in Romans 6:13 when he writes 'if you live according to the flesh you will die, but if by the Spirit you put to death the deeds of the body you will die.'

As we have seen earlier in this chapter, the 'works of the flesh' which we are called to turn away from in the power of the Spirit take multiple forms, but among these is the rejection by transgender people of the sexual identity which God has given to them and which is determined by the sex of their body.

This means that in the case of a transgender person who is a baptised believer the call to put off the old nature and put on the new one has to mean, among other things, being willing to accept and live out their true, God given, sexual identity. For those going through gender transition this will mean stopping the process and for those who have gone through gender transition this will mean undergoing de-transition and reverting to living according to their birth sex.

Good pastoral care will mean explaining theologically to the person concerned why this course of action is called for as part of their new life in Christ and journeying with them as they seek to live it out. It will also mean advising the person concerned to seek appropriate psychiatric help as and when necessary to help deal with any unresolved psychiatric issues which either lie behind the person's gender dysphoria or arise from it.

If those who have gone through gender transition have a family life in their assumed identity pastoral care will also need to involve helping to address the relationship issues which will arise as a result of their return to their true identity (an example of what this might means in practice is given in appendix 3 at the end of this report).

It is easy to outline these aspects of pastoral care for transgender people in writing. Putting them into practice will, of course be immensely more difficult. As the Evangelical Alliance report on transsexuality correctly notes: 'The pathway of growth, sanctification and change can be expected to be slow and painful. Struggle and relapse can be anticipated.'[19] The desire to live as a member of the other sex may never go away in this life, even if it lessens or can be controlled, and the psychological, emotional and practical issues involved in giving up a legal public identity as a member of one sex and reverting to another sex will be immense and will take time to resolve. Those who have undergone sex reassignment surgery may have to learn to live with the fact that some aspects of what have happened to them are irreversible and that they will have mutilated bodies for the rest of their lives.

Furthermore, in a culture which is increasingly supportive of gender transition there will be constant cultural influences suggesting that it would be desirable to continue to live in their assumed identity and in addition, as the Evangelical Alliance report explains: 'Fellow transsexuals will usually be convinced that change is not possible and sometimes seek to dissuade someone seeking in this way to be obedient to Christ.' [20]

---

[19] The Evangelical Alliance, *Transsexuality* (Carlisle: Paternoster Press, 2000), p 82.
[20] The Evangelical Alliance, *Transsexuality*, p 83.

Supporting people through this range of difficulties will be a major challenge for a minister and for a congregation. What it will mean in practice is a long term commitment to praying for and loving, listening to and assisting the person concerned in any way necessary. It will also mean continuing to love and support them even if progress is slow and relapses occur, trusting that God is in the process and has the capacity to bring about the result that he desires even if this takes years. As Walt Heyer reminds us in *A Transgender's Faith*: '...we must never give up on people, no matter how many times they fail or how long recovery takes. We must never underestimate the healing power of prayer and love in the hands of the Lord. We must never give up hope.'[21]

Understanding that sanctification is a long term and complex process and that it is a result of the new life in the Spirit that comes about through faith and baptism provides a right perspective on a number of issues.

First, it means that when a transgender person first comes to church and is present in their assumed sexual identity they need to be welcomed as they are even if it is known that their identity is one that has been assumed. It would be completely inappropriate to expect them to change as a condition of welcome. Like everyone else, they should be welcomed unconditionally.[22]

Secondly, it means that it would be inappropriate to refuse to baptise someone because they have not yet reverted to their true identity. It is true that repentance and faith are required of those who are baptised, but insisting that repentance has to take the specific form of reverting to living according to one's birth sex would arguably be to prematurely demand sanctification as pre-condition for spiritual re-generation rather than look for it as a fruit of such re-generation.

Thirdly, it means that if someone who is a baptised believer is unwilling to contemplate reverting to their true sexual identity, or comes to believe that they the only way they can achieve a degree of psychological wholeness is by going through a process of sex

---

[21] Heyer, *A Transgender's Faith*, p 141.

[22] This observation provides the right context for considering specific issues such as the use of toilet facilities. In considering this or other issues the question to ask is always what will provide a welcome for someone in the current stage of their life. It also means that it is appropriate to refer to someone who has undergone gender transition by their assumed name and identity until they choose to change them. As with any other form of pastoral care it is important to begin where people are and move on from there.

re-assignment surgery then we should stick with them for the long term. Obviously it would be wrong not to explain to them why doing either would mean going against God's will, but if they still persist then we need to continue to love them, support them, and pray that they will eventually by brought by God to see the truth about who they truly are and how they should live.

5. Should we vote for the Blackburn motion?

As we saw in the introduction, the motion put forward to General Synod by Blackburn diocese is as follows:

That this Synod, recognising the need for transgender people to be welcomed and affirmed in their parish church, calls on the House of Bishops to consider whether some nationally commended liturgical materials might be prepared to mark a person's gender transition.

As we also saw in chapter 1, if this motion were to be passed and then implemented it would mean that the Church of England as a whole accepted the claim that someone can be a woman with male biology and vice versa.

The question we have considered in the remainder of this report is whether it would be right to accept this claim. What has become clear in the course of this consideration is the answer to this question is 'no' for two reasons.

First, as we have seen, the arguments that have been put forward in support of gender transition are unpersuasive:

a) It does not makes theological sense to claim that the transcendent creator God of the Bible is either intersex or transgender.

b) It is inconsistent with a belief in God's goodness to say that he has deliberately created people who have an incongruity between their perception of their sexual identity and the sexual identity of their bodies.

c) There is no convincing scientific evidence to support the idea that people who are transgender have a brain that is of the opposite sex to that of their bodies and is in line with their perception of their sexual identity.

d) It is not clear why we should accept the claim that transgender people make about their sexual identity given that we would not accept a similar claim about someone's race or species. 'I say I am X' is not in itself a convincing argument.

e) The idea that someone can have a sexual identity that is the opposite to that of their body is incoherent. To be male or female has to do with the sex of a person's body. The claim that someone's self is male or female when that self has no corresponding male or female body thus does not make any sense.

f) The claim that gender transition is the best way to help someone with gender dysphoria is called into question by the available evidence which fails to demonstrate that transition is successful in resolving the mental and physical health issues experienced by transgender people. Scepticism about gender transition is expressed both by well qualified experts in the field of mental health and by a growing number of people who are explaining the reasons why, having gone through gender transition, they then decided to revert back to living in their birth sex.

g) The idea that someone can have a sexual identity that is opposite to that of their body is inconsistent with the creation narratives in Genesis 1 and 2 and with the anthropology of the Bible as a whole. These teach us that God has created human beings as embodied creatures who are either male or female dependent upon the nature of their embodiment and that their God given vocation to reproduce is fulfilled by men reproducing as fathers and women as mothers.

h) The Biblical account of creation does not leave space for people who are neither male nor female and what we know about intersex conditions tells us that people who have these conditions are not a third sex, but someone whose body has developed in a way that is disordered in some way so that it is not either male or female in the way that human bodies are meant to be.

i) The idea that eunuchs are biblical role models for the acceptance of gender transition falls foul of the fact that eunuchs in the Bible are simply men who cannot have children, either because of disease, castration or voluntary celibacy.

j) The fact that the language used to describe the Church in the New Testament mixes male and female imagery does not negate the fact that the New Testament consistently makes a distinction between men and women. Likewise, Galatians 3:28 does not teach that the sexual distinction between men and women has been abolished in Christ, but rather teaches that both men and women alike can receive through faith the blessing promised to Abraham.

k) The biblical vision of a renewed creation and its account of the resurrection of the dead do not give support to gender transition because the Bible teaches that when creation is renewed we shall inhabit God's kingdom with the same sexed bodies we have at present albeit animated by God's Spirit and thereby rendered immortal.

l) The change in people's names in the Bible (as in Abram to Abraham or Simon to Peter) is never linked to a change in sexual identity.

m) The prohibition of cross dressing in Deuteronomy 22:5 is relevant to the transgender issue because it expresses the principle that in accordance with creation men should live as men and women as women, a principle reiterated in the New Testament in 1 Corinthians 11:2-16.

n) The fact that Jesus was miraculously born of the Virgin Mary through the action of the Holy Spirit does not mean that he was intersex, the fact that he was 'queer' in the sense of nonconforming does not mean that he rejected the Jewish belief in the distinction between men and women (an idea for which there is no evidence) and the fact that he was both human and divine and went through a series of changes or 'transitions' in the course of his ministry does not mean that there are people who are somehow in essence both male and female or that gender transition is theologically acceptable.

o) Those who oppose gender transition should not be seen as being like Job's comforters. Job's comforters spoke untruthfully about God while those opposed to the concept of gender transition are truthfully describing how God has created human beings and desires that they should live.

Secondly, as we have also seen, there is an alternative and preferable Christian framework for looking at the phenomenon of gender transition and the appropriate way to offer pastoral care for transgender people.

This framework starts off by noting that both the Bible and the study of nature teach us that human beings have been created as bodily creatures who are either male or female depending on how their bodies are formed for the purpose of sexual reproduction.

This basic bodily distinction between male and female, which the Bible teaches will continue in the world to come, can be seen, in accordance with the teaching of Genesis 1:31, as something that is 'very good' because (a) the ability to sexually reproduce allows the human race to survive and (b) sexual desire, sexual reproduction and the institution of marriage associated with them, point us to the passionate, fruitful and faithful nature of God's love for us and all creation and to our communion with God in the world to come as the ultimate fulfilment of all our earthly desires.

These things being so, the calling of human beings is to accept with gratitude God's creation of us as either men or women and to live faithfully before God as either men or women as created.

This calling is challenged by those secular and theological voices who argue that human beings should move beyond the 'gender binary' of men and women either to a world in which there are multiple forms of sexual identity or to a totally sexless form of human existence. This form of thinking is an example of the primary sin of trying to be like God by determining for ourselves what human existence should be like (eating of 'the fruit of the tree of the knowledge of good and evil' Genesis 2:17).

Those who undergo gender transition do not reject the distinction between men and women, but they do believe that their true sex is different from that of their bodies and that they should seek to live according to their true sex, changing their bodies where necessary in order to try to achieve this.

From a Christian theological perspective this belief and the action that flows from it have to be seen as a manifestation of human sinfulness. According to biblical teaching, all human beings are sinners as a consequence of the sin of Adam and this means that they have a fallen nature which manifests itself in wrong thinking, wrong desiring and wrong acting. In the case of those involved in gender transition this means specifically a wrong belief that they have a sex which is different from that of their body, a wrong desire to live as a member of that sex and wrong acting in trying to bring that about instead of living as the person God made them to be.

Pastoral care for transgender people needs to start off by welcoming them unconditionally as those made in God's image whom he cares for as a widow cares for a lost coin, a shepherd cares for a lost sheep and father cares for a lost son (Luke 15:1-32). However it cannot stop there.

Transgender people, just like all other human beings, are enslaved by the world, the flesh and the Devil and are subject to judgement and eternal death. However, God in his great mercy has acted to deliver them from their captivity and to raise them to a new life with Christ, a new life which is received through faith and baptism. Pastoral care therefore has to mean not only welcoming transgender people, but seeking to ensure that they believe and are baptised. This is the top spiritual priority that needs to precede addressing the issue of their sexual identity.

Nonetheless, because those who have been given new life have to live it out in obedience to God in the power of the Spirit this issue does need to be addressed. Living out the new life Christ has given them has to mean for transgender people seeking to live as the people God made them to be. Pastoral care therefore means seeking to help people either not to go through with gender transition or to revert to living according to their true sex if they have done so. This will be a hard road to travel and ministers and congregations have to be prepared to travel it with them, however long it takes, and even if there are relapses on the way.

Because the arguments for the acceptance of gender transition are unpersuasive, and in the light of this alternative way of looking at the issue, it would clearly be wrong to vote yes to the Blackburn motion.

To develop and commend a form of liturgy to mark gender transition would mean:

- The Church of England declaring untruthfully to those both inside and outside the Church that someone's true sex can be different from the sex of their body.

- The Church of England failing to make clear to those inside and outside the Church that undergoing gender transition is something that is contrary to God's will and so should not be undertaken, however desirable it might seem.

- The Church of England failing to make clear to those inside and outside the Church that both theology and non-theological research show us that a process of gender transition is not the best way forward for those with gender dysphoria and that a better approach is a combination of pastoral care allied with psychiatric support where needed to help people to learn to live as members of the sex into which they were born.

These are three things that the Church of England must not do and so the Blackburn proposal needs to be rejected.

Instead, the Church of England needs (a) to produce clear teaching explaining the nature of our sexual identity and why this is a good gift from God and (b) to develop the resources which are at the moment sadly lacking to help clergy and others provide transgender people with effective pastoral care.

6. Additional Material

6.1. Appendix 1: The Lutheran Church – Missouri Synod Gender Identity Disorder or Gender Dysphoria in Christian Perspective[1]

"Gender" has become a matter of uncertainty. Rather than male or female, many see gender as a relative matter, or even a continuum. They consider gender or sexual identity to be less a reality given at conception than a matter of personal discovery.[2] Reflective of such a theoretical perspective, increasing attention is also given to individuals who are personally uncertain about their own gender or sexual identity – in particular, individuals who are "transsexual" or "transgendered,"[3] as well as those who identify themselves as "bisexual" or are "questioning" their gender and in the process of determining what they perceive to be their true gender identity.[4]

In recent years the Commission on Theology and Church Relations has been asked about the specific matter of transsexual or transgendered individuals. Questions have come from individuals with personal questions about sexual identity including persons who are

---

[1] As Lutheran Christians, a consideration of The Lutheran Church—Missouri Synod on this and any topic is grounded in belief in the full authority of Holy Scripture as God's infallible Word and the conviction that the Confessions of the Lutheran Church are a truthful interpretation of the Scriptures. The general perspective of this report, however, is one that is not simply that of the Lutheran theological tradition, but rather stands within the broad (catholic) consensus of traditional Christian teaching.

[2] This is an element of what is sometimes referred to in gender studies as the "social constructionism" movement in psychological theory. As an example, see Rachel Alsop, et al., *Theorizing Gender: An Introduction* (Malden, Massachusetts: Blackwell Publishers, 2002).

[3] For the purposes of this document, the definitions of transsexual and transgender used by the American Psychiatric Association are utilized. See the text below under Psychotherapeutic Considerations for those definitions (p 88).

[4] Note the familiar acronym LGBT (Lesbian, Gay, Bisexual, Transgendered) to which is now frequently added Q for Questioning – LGBTQ. Both acronyms are regularly present not only in secular discussions, but also in ecclesial settings. Ecclesial LGBT(Q) lobbies have pressed church bodies to make changes allowing ordination into the ministry and religious blessing of same-sex unions or marriages of practicing homosexual persons. Such lobbies are also advocates for Bisexual and Transgendered individuals and others who are Questioning their sexual identity.

uncertain whether they are "truly" male or female, others who are regularly dressing and presenting themselves as a member of the opposite sex, and still others who are participating in hormonal or surgical procedures to change their sex identification from male to female or from female to male. In addition to concerns from individuals questioning their sexual identity, church workers have asked for guidance in pastoral care for individuals struggling with matters of gender identity.

The following pages will consider, first, some of the current psychotherapeutic perspectives of the American Psychiatric Association. Those perspectives are important, yet Christian churches seek a theological understanding as grounded in the higher authority of God's revelation in Scripture. Thus the remainder of the report provides theological reflection on the topic of sexual identity and suggestions for pastoral care.

6.1.1. Psychotherapeutic Considerations

The American Psychiatric Association's (APA) 1994 *Diagnostic and Statistical Manual of Mental Disorders*, 4th Edition (*DSM-IV*) listed four criteria required for a person to be diagnosed with gender identity disorder (i.e., as a transsexual or transgendered individual): Strong and persistent cross-gender identification; Persistent discomfort about one's assigned sex or a sense of inappropriateness in the gender-role of that sex; The individual does not have a concurrent physical intersex condition [hermaphroditism[5]]; Clinically significant distress or impairment in social, occupational, or other important areas of functioning.[6]

In recent years, these criteria and the APA's 1994 categorization of the condition as a "disorder" have stirred controversy within the psychotherapeutic community together with impassioned debate. The primary concern that many have had with *DSM-IV* has been the assumption that identifying with a gender other than the one assigned at birth is a "disorder." The label "disorder" is thought to imply a value judgment. For example, the doctor who chaired the gender identity disorder committee of the APA has been criticized by many because he

---

5   A hermaphrodite is a person having both male and female sexual tissues. It is an older term for a condition now included under the term "intersex" which is defined in the body of this section or described by the phrase "disorder of sex development" (DSD).

6   *DSM-IV* (Washington, DC: American Psychiatric Association, 1994) 537-538.

advocates cognitive behavioral treatment for the disorder in children (although he does not advocate such treatment for adults).[7]

As a result of the debate the most recent edition of the *Diagnostic and Statistical Manual of Mental Disorders*, 5th Edition (*DSM-5*[8]), released in May of 2013, discontinued the term "gender identity disorder" in favor of "gender dysphoria."[9] *DSM-5* distinguishes between gender dysphoria in children and adults. It defines "transgender" persons as those "who transiently or persistently identify with a gender different from their natal gender" and "transsexual" persons as those who either seek or have undergone "a social transition from male to female or female to male" whether or not that entails hormonal or surgical treatments.[10] *DSM-5* continues to maintain a distinction between sexual dysphoria and an intersex condition (in which an individual has physically or genetically ambiguous sexual traits). "Overall, current evidence is insufficient to label gender dysphoria without a disorder of sex development as a form of intersexuality limited to the central nervous system."[11]

Gender dysphoria in both children and adults is reportedly more prevalent in males than in females. For adults identified as male at birth, the incidence reported in *DSM-5* is between 0.005% to 0.014% (5-14 cases in every 100,000 males). For adults identified as female at

---

7   Dr. Kenneth Zucker is a sexologist who specializes in the care of children with gender dysphoria. He favors cognitive behavioral therapy only in children and disavows reparative therapy for homosexuals. "Kenneth Zucker." Wikipedia, The Free Encyclopedia. <http://en.wikipedia.org/wiki/Kenneth_Zucker> (accessed: 29 October 2013). Cognitive behavioral therapy in this context may be generally defined as a therapeutic process that attempts to help an individuals change their sexual identity. In this case, Zucker's approach seeks to help children who are identifying with the opposite sex to be accepting of their own sex as a boy or girl.

8   *DSM-IV* and predecessor editions were identified by Roman numerals when abbreviated. DSM-5 uses the Arabic numeral.

9   *DSM-5* (Arlington, Virginia: American Psychiatric Association, 2013), 451-459. Dysphoria is medically defined as "an emotional state marked by anxiety, depression, and restlessness" (dysphoria. Dictionary.com. The American Heritage® Stedman's Medical Dictionary. Houghton Mifflin Company. http://dictionary. reference.com/browse/dysphoria [accessed: 29 October 2013]). 10 *DSM-5*, 451.

10   *DSM-5*, 451.

11   *DSM-5*, 457. In other words, there is insufficient evidence to suggest that gender dysphoria has a biological cause unless it is accompanied by sexual ambiguity of a physical nature (intersex condition or DSD). *DSM-5* cites evidence that hormonal levels for natal males with sexual dysphoria are similar to those for the male population without sexual dysphoria. Hormonal levels for natal females with sexual dysphoria indicate a slightly higher, but statistically insignificant, level of testosterone than found in the average female population.

birth, the rate is from 0.002-0.003% (2-3 cases in every 100,000 females). No global prevalence data is offered for gender dysphoria in children, but the ratio from many international studies again suggests a greater rate of occurrence in boys compared to girls (between 2 and 4.5 times as often for boys as for girls). In a final note on prevalence, however, *DSM-5* indicates that Japan and Poland report more sexual dysphoria in females than in males.[12] (No further information on any of the data is given and *DSM-5* does not indicate either the sources of the research or its sample populations.)

In an online pamphlet released in advance of *DSM-5*, gender dysphoria is described as follows:

> For a person to be diagnosed with gender dysphoria, there must be a marked difference between the individual's expressed/experienced gender and the gender others would assign him or her, and it must continue for at least six months. In children, the desire to be of the other gender must be present and verbalized. This condition causes clinically significant distress or impairment in social, occupational, or other important areas of functioning.
>
> Gender dysphoria is manifested in a variety of ways, including strong desires to be treated as the other gender or to be rid of one's sex characteristics, or a strong conviction that one has feelings and reactions typical of the other gender.[13]

DSM-5 itself states: "Gender dysphoria refers to the distress that may accompany the incongruence between one's experienced or expressed gender and one's assigned gender." It furthermore indicates that "[t]he current term is more descriptive than the previous *DSM-IV* term gender identity disorder and focuses on dysphoria as the clinical problem, not identity per se."[14] In taking this stance, the APA is acknowledging both the afore-mentioned debate and also the complexity of the research that has been conducted in this area. While an intersex condition (see below) is rather distinctive and clearly involves biological and genetic criteria, the causes of individual distress over one's apparent sex – one's "natal gender"[15] – are highly complex. There is no certain physiological or genetic cause for such dysphoria.

---

[12]   *DSM-5*, 454.

[13]   See http://www.dsm5.org/Documents/Gender%20Dysphoria%20Fact%20Sheet.pdf (accessed 29 Oct. 2013).

[14]   *DSM-5*, 451; emphases in the original.

[15]   The term "natal gender" is used and defined in *DSM-5*, 451 as the identity associated with biological indicators that is given to an individual at birth.

The change in terminology from *DSM-IV* to *DSM-5* is significant because it indicates a reluctance to identify the confusion that an individual may feel about whether he or she is male or female, despite his or her natal gender, as a clinical problem. Rather than an identity disorder, *DSM-5* only recognizes the distress the individual feels as a treatable problem. This suggests that the debate with its consequent conceptual and terminological changes has occurred in large measure because a value judgment is perceived to be at the heart of the notion that cross-gender identification is itself a "disorder" and therefore detrimental or negative.

Viewing sexual identity from a perspective of ordered or disordered implies a moral judgment, with "good" versus "bad" implied. Such moral reflection has been progressively excluded from the fields of psychology and psychiatry in recent decades. The elimination of homosexuality from the list of psychiatric disorders on December 15, 1973 is a relevant example. That elimination was grounded primarily in the conviction that it was a moral value judgment to declare homosexuality a psychiatric disorder that should be treated.

The continuing debate regarding homosexual conduct in the United States is in large measure a debate between a biblical and traditionally Christian understanding of the moral quality of homosexual behavior and the understanding, adopted by an increasing percentage of those in the psychiatric community since 1973, that homosexuality is either a natural condition or a valid lifestyle alternative. The underlying question is whether there is space for moral judgment in determining human behavior that requires psychiatric or psychological therapeutic care. The trajectory of past thinking and current *DSM* judgments indicates a similar perspective about matters of gender identity, namely, that such dysphoria should not be viewed in any way that involves moral judgment. The APA therefore approaches such an issue from a significantly different standpoint than the standpoint of Christian theology.

6.1.2. *Christian Moral Reflection on Gender Identity*

Christian theological and moral reflection on matters of gender identity must note the trajectory indicated above and its basis in the 1973 decision of the APA. An underlying assumption of those who press for changes in the church's understanding of homosexual behavior has been that one's embodiment should not be a determinative factor in moral behavior. In other words, simply because one is physically male, he should not have to accept that the natural and God-pleasing sexual expression appropriate to him should be toward females. And, if one is physically female, she should not feel morally compelled to restrict any sexual desires for women. Similarly, one who has sexual desire for both men and women, should not seek to deny such desires or feel compelled to restrict his or her sexual contact only to the opposite sex. And, lastly, just because one has male genitalia, one should not be encouraged to seek treatment for the fact that one feels more like a female.

The entire Christian tradition and the majority of Christian churches today have opposed such changes in perspective. The basis for such opposition is precisely because our embodiment is understood as an aspect of our creation by God and therefore instructive regarding behavior that is good and pleasing to Him. Human embodiment indicates simply and eloquently God's intention for sexual activity – that male and female by becoming "one flesh" might end their aloneness in lifelong unity with one another and, according to God's blessing, in the procreation of children (Gen 1:26-28; Gen 2:18-24). Homosexual or bisexual desire and activity is therefore viewed as aberrant (see Gen 19:4-11; Lev 18:22; 20:13; Rom 1:24-27; 1 Cor 6:9; and 1 Tim 1:10), because it contradicts the meaning and purpose of one's embodiment as male or female.

This biblical view is not unrealistic about human nature in a fallen world. It is true that one result of sin is that desires and behavior become disordered. Husbands and wives inevitably experience (and too frequently act out) sexual desire for men and women other than their spouses. In other cases, men and women experience (and frequently act out) desire for individuals of their same sex.

The very same line of thought would apply to one who is embodied as a man but feels persistent discomfort with his maleness or for a person with a female body who believes she is male. From the standpoint of our bodies – which is the only objective means of determining who is male or female – we have a God-given identity that is either masculine or feminine. One is a man or a woman because that is what the body given by God indicates.[16]

Christian theology has consistently sought to distinguish desires and feelings from behavior. Greed, rage, jealousy, resentment, arrogance, depression, and the many shapes that lust can take are but a few examples of feelings or desires that every human experiences to

---

[16] This does not deny the reality of situations in which there is sexual ambiguity that is physical or biological in nature. See the excursus on Intersex below for further consideration of biological sexual ambiguity.

various degrees and at various times. Such desires are part of fallen human nature itself (e.g., Gal 5:17 or 1 John 2:16), but they are to be opposed and curbed, rather than to be given free reign (Rom 13:14). The Christian theological tradition has therefore sought always to distinguish between desires and acting out desires, and between specific behavioral sins and the sinner. It recognizes that in our fallen humanity, behavior can be disciplined to some degree, while inner feelings are far less subject to human control.

Christianity understands homosexuality, bisexuality, or transgendered identity and desire within such an overall moral framework. It seeks to follow natural law (the objective truth of our bodies) and the revealed truth of Holy Scriptures, even if the truth these sources convey conflicts with societal or professional opinions, such as that of psychology or psychiatry.

One response to such reflection is that, while there is scriptural direction which clearly forbids homosexual activity, there is no explicit scriptural reference to transgendered individuals. There are only references that hint at implications for the individual who feels discomfort with his or her identity as male or female.[17]

Jesus, however, grounds sexual morality not only in revelatory truth, but also in our created nature (see Matt 19:1-9). When he condemns divorce, he does so because, from the very beginning, "the Creator" (NIV; "he who created them" NAS ESV NRSV) has made us male and female (Matt 19:4). Jesus points to our creation as male and female and therefore endorses the conclusion that "a man shall leave his father and mother, be united to his wife, and the two become one flesh," quoting Genesis 2:24. As one flesh, the man and woman have been joined by God and should not separate.

Paul speaks within the same context of male and female and the same foundational passage from Genesis in his teaching on marriage

---

[17] There is, indeed, no explicit mention, much less extended discussion per se in the Bible, of transsexual or transgendered persons or persons experiencing distress over their physical sexual embodiment. Deuteronomy 22:5 is, however, a strong condemnation of wearing the garments of the opposite sex. Some argue that such an Old Testament reference has no applicability to Christians. A more classical Christian interpretation is that this verse represents an example of "moral law" with continuing applicability. Moreover, St. Paul's reference to "effeminates" in 1 Cor 6:9 (New American Standard and King James Version; the New International Version translates the term as "male prostitutes") is a likely reference to individual men who "cultivate feminine features." Cf. Robert A. J. Gagnon, *The Bible and Homosexual Practice: Texts and Hermeneutics* (Nashville: Abingdon Press, 2001), 307-308.

(Eph 5:22-33). And as he further discusses sexual morality in marital and unmarried life (cf. 1 Cor 6:12-7:40), he does so from within a perspective that acknowledges our created embodiment as male and female ("glorify God in your body," 1 Cor 6:20), the expectation of sexual self-control whether married or unmarried (1 Cor 6:18; 7:5, 9), the call to live the life we have been given (vocation, 1 Cor 7:17, 24), and the priority of serving God in our daily lives (1 Cor 7:32).

The reasoning of Scripture regarding our sexual nature is therefore inarguable. In addition to the previous passages, Paul's discussion of homosexuality in Romans 1 is important. He considers homosexual acts in the context of one particular trait of human sin: the suppression of the truth (Rom 1:18). He gives two examples of suppressing truth. The first is our refusal to acknowledge the divine power and nature which alone could bring about the created world, which results in humans worshiping creatures instead of the Creator (Rom 1:19-23, also v. 25). Paul's second example results from the first: because we worship the creation and not the Creator, we are also given to dishonoring our bodies rather than seeking the will of the Creator for their proper use. This, Paul says, is the reason humanity is even willing to ignore the obvious intention of our creation as male and female and exchange "natural relations for those that are contrary to nature" as women engage in sexual relations with other women and men engage in sexual relations with other men (Rom 1:24-27). Paul's understanding of the immorality of homosexual activity is grounded in our created nature as sexual beings, our embodiment as man or woman, and is not understood as an arbitrary moral rule revealed by God.

Moreover, within the Lutheran theological tradition, one may note the relevance of the explanation of the first article of the Creed by Martin Luther. Having confessed, "I believe in God the Father almighty, maker of heaven and earth," Luther's answer to the question, "What does this mean?" is directly applicable to this discussion: "I believe that God has made me and all creatures, that He has given me my body and soul, eyes, ears, *and all my members....*"[18]

---

[18] Emphasis added. The translation of the Small Catechism is from Luther's *Small Catechism with Explanation* (Saint Louis, Concordia Publishing House, 1998, 2005), 15. Cp. Robert Kolb and Timothy J. Wengert, eds., *The Book of Concord: Confessions of the Evangelical Lutheran Church* (Minneapolis: Fortress Press, 2000), 354, which reads "all limbs" rather than members, in translating the German *Glieder*. The term *Glied*, however, is used to refer to all body parts. Moreover, the Latin version of the Small Catechism reads *"omnia membra"* for the text in question.

To declare faith in the work of God's creation in our lives is to confess that our bodies, with all their parts – including our sexual organs[19] – are given to us by God our heavenly Father. The parts of the body are arranged and appointed "each one of them, as he chose" (1 Cor 12:18). It is from this consideration of the creation of the human body with all its members that the inspired apostle then develops the rich and beautiful image of the church as the body of Christ with all its members.

A biblical approach to sexual morality, therefore, is not simply grounded in specific Bible passages alone. It is grounded, first, in the truth of our nature as created beings ("natural law") as that is understood in Scripture. From this standpoint, the Christian understanding of confused sexual identity is clear. Because Christianity takes our created bodies seriously, it is compelled to view it as a disorder of creation if a man or woman feels discomfort with his or her body and desires either to dress and act in the manner of the opposite sex or to "change" his or her sex by means of hormones or surgery. Ultimately, such feelings or actions are fruitless violations of our nature. Such surgery, for example, will not change the individual's chromosomal makeup, but will only mutilate the body God has given.

6.1.3. Excursus: Intersex Condition as an Area of Special Concern

One special area of concern must be discussed in this context. *DSM-IV* criteria (above) explicitly excluded from the diagnosis of sexual identity disorder individuals with "intersex" condition, but such persons should not be forgotten in a Christian moral and pastoral discussion of gender dysphoria. An intersex condition in humans can take two forms, one in which both male and female gonads are present at birth and the individual has both male (XY) and female (XX) chromosomes. The second form involves the chromosomes and gonads of one sex but the physical appearance of the opposite sex.[20] As noted above, *DSM-5* maintains a distinction between intersexuality and sexual dysphoria.

---

[19] Perhaps Paul's reference to our "unpresentable parts" in 1 Corinthians 12:23 is worth mentioning. The context of 1 Corinthians 12 is one in which he affirms the richness of the body of Christ by means of analogy to the human body, the parts of which, are all afforded high regard and worth. That includes the sexual "members" of the body which, while treated with modesty, are nonetheless worthy of equal regard to eyes, ears, noses, hands, and feet which are ever active and noticeable. See Gregory J. Lockwood, *1 Corinthians* (Saint Louis: Concordia Publishing House, 2000), 446-447, for a discussion of the "inferior" members of the body.

[20] "hermaphroditism." *Encyclopædia Britannica*. 2013. Encyclopædia Britannica Online. Accessed 29 Oct. 2013 http://www.britannica.com/EBchecked/topic/263151/hermaphroditism.

All creation displays the results of sin and death, even though God created the world to be a place of goodness and life. Such is the sobering assessment of Christian reflection on the fall into sin. Congenital disorders and other examples of nature in rebellion against humanity, of which an intersex condition would be an example, are understood from a Christian theological perspective as examples of creation in "bondage to corruption" as a result of the corrupting force of the fall into sin (see Gen 3:16-19; Rom 8:20-23).

While an individual with hermaphroditic features may not fit the concept of gender identity disorder (by *DSM-IV's* standard) or the concept of being transgendered, such a person will likely know some measure of distress or dysphoria and might well seek pastoral guidance and direction. Here the guidance would be more dependent upon medical advice than any particular scriptural position. The fundamental Christian perspective would be to encourage treatment of the condition in a way that allows the greatest possible fullness of service to Christ and others by the individual. This may well entail hormonal or surgical options that enable the person to deal most effectively with the biological sexual ambiguity which is present.

6.1.4. Pastoral Care for Gender Identity Confusion

A pastoral response to individuals with any form of gender dysphoria requires a clear grounding in a biblically based understanding of natural law and our creation by God as male and female. A biblical understanding of both the gravity of sin's effects and the Gospel of redemption from sin by grace through faith in Jesus Christ is also necessary. But such doctrinal awareness is not the sum of pastoral care. The church's ministry is instead always anchored in the responsibility to proclaim, reflect, and enact the love of God in Christ Jesus – his love for a fallen world – in the lives of specific individuals.

The pastor will understand that the person who is struggling with sexual identity is indeed dealing with a grave disorder, but he will also understand that the deepest need of such a man or woman – as it is for every person – is to know that he or she is beloved by God. Christ's love and forgiveness are in this case as always one's greatest needs. Sorrow, confusion, frustration, shame, and despair are likely present in any individual dealing with gender dysphoria or struggling with questions about his or her identity as male or female. If such an individual has not already sought psychotherapeutic care, the pastor should seek to encourage and, to whatever degree possible, facilitate the individual in securing competent therapy that is not hostile to the Christian faith.[21]

While it is unlikely that the pastor is trained or equipped to serve as a therapist for this condition, the value of pastoral care and counsel should not be minimized. The pastor has the opportunity to provide compassionate care anchored in the Word of God – care that recognizes both the power of sin and the even stronger, gracious acceptance of our Lord Jesus for humanity despite our sins and weaknesses (Mark 9:17-27; Luke 19:10).

Pastoral care for such a person struggling with sexual identity does not begin with debates about what is or is not moral. Certainly, the Christian pastor is called to help an individual struggling with sexual identity to understand the biblical view of human sexuality and to distinguish between his or her feelings and actions based on those feelings. The rightfully persistent idea of loving the sinner even as one discourages specific sins is vital here as it is in every situation of pastoral care and moral guidance.

More important for pastoral care, however, is the development of genuine Christian friendship modeled after the One whose friendship knows no boundaries (Luke 7:34). Loving pastoral care for the individual seeks to provide a spiritually nurturing, encouraging, and accepting "safe place" to someone who may well have suffered from actual or perceived ostracism, mockery, and animosity. He or she may view the church with suspicion or share the common assumption that Christianity is more concerned with moral judgments, cultural battles, or political victories than about broken and suffering people. In accepting the struggling individual, a relationship of interpersonal trust develops. Within that relationship there will be natural opportunities to make Christ known, to call the person to trust in his promises and love, and to show that the purposes and commands of God for our lives are for our good.

Pastoral care in such circumstances will be challenging, to put it mildly. Individuals who have had sexual reassignment procedures and then come to the conviction that their actions were mistakes and were

---

[21] It would be good for every pastor to know of therapists who are clinically competent to provide therapy to individuals in need. That may not always be easily accomplished. It is true that there are some therapists who are suspicious of or even hostile to the Christian faith and biblical teaching, particularly with respect to sexual morality. A pastor may wish to consult with the American Association of Christian Counselors. (http://www.aacc.net/resources/find-a-counselor/).

not God-pleasing will need special care and encouragement.[22] In addition to encouraging competent therapy (as noted above), the work of pastoral care for a such persons will seek to treat their immediate spiritual needs, dividing Law and Gospel with care and helping them to accept what may well be a permanent, difficult reality (cf. 2 Cor 12:7-9). Specific strategies for working toward a renewed and God-pleasing life will differ from case to case. In such cases it may be advisable for the pastor to seek permission to discuss the case with the individual's therapist. At all times, communicating the important truth of God's persisting love for us, no matter what we have done in and to our lives, is the center of the pastor's care.

If the pastor is caring for a person who is struggling with sexual identity but rejects the Christian church's guidance in this matter, the pastoral task is similar to many other instances of pastoral care in the face of sin and fallenness. Admonition and the call to repentance are needed; some measure of Christian discipline may also become necessary. Pastors regularly require patience in both holding to the truth of God's Word while just as patiently seeking to provide loving support as they seek to bring to repentance those who do not see that truth clearly or are otherwise inclined to reject it. Support and counsel from others, including fellow clergy and others who are in ministry, is vital to the pastor. This also includes seeking guidance from Christians who work in the mental health professions.

In closing, the important pastoral tool of individual confession and absolution should not be neglected, but coupled with pastoral counsel and genuine Christian friendship. Nothing is more powerful in the life of every person – for all of us fallen people – than the forgiveness that is given through the suffering and death of our Lord Jesus. It is the greatest responsibility and privilege of pastoral care to proclaim Christ's forgiveness, freely and graciously given, and received simply by faith in our Lord's promises.

Adopted Saturday, May 17, 2014 Commission on Theology and Church Relations

The Lutheran Church—Missouri Synod

---

[22] There have been a few cases when transsexuals engaged in further medical procedures to attempt to restore the physical traits of their natal gender. However, that will often be an unrealistic if not impossible goal.

6.2. Appendix 2: On Transgender Identity – Southern Baptist Convention Baltimore, MD – 2014

WHEREAS, All persons are created in God's image and are made to glorify Him (Genesis 1:27; Isaiah 43:7); and

WHEREAS, God's design was the creation of two distinct and complementary sexes, male and female (Genesis 1:27; Matthew 19:4; Mark 10:6) which designate the fundamental distinction that God has embedded in the very biology of the human race; and

WHEREAS, Distinctions in masculine and feminine roles as ordained by God are part of the created order and should find expression in every human heart (Genesis 2:18, 21-24; 1 Corinthians 11:7-9; Ephesians 5:22-33; 1 Timothy 2:12-14); and

WHEREAS, The Fall of man into sin and God's subsequent curse have introduced brokenness and futility into God's good creation (Genesis 3:1-24; Romans 8:20); and

WHEREAS, According to a 2011 survey, about 700,000 Americans perceive their gender identity to be at variance with the physical reality of their biological birth sex; and

WHEREAS, Transgenderism differs from hermaphroditism or intersexualism in that the sex of the individual is not biologically ambiguous but psychologically ambiguous; and

WHEREAS, The American Psychiatric Association removed this condition (aka, "gender identity disorder") from its list of disorders in 2013, substituting "gender identity disorder" with "gender dysphoria"; and

WHEREAS, The American Psychiatric Association includes among its treatment options for gender dysphoria cross-sex hormone therapy, gender reassignment surgery, and social and legal transition to the desired gender; and

WHEREAS, News reports indicate that parents are allowing their children to undergo these therapies; and

WHEREAS, Many LGBT activists have sought to normalize the transgender experience and to define gender according to one's self-perception apart from biological anatomy; and

WHEREAS, The separation of one's gender identity from the physical reality of biological birth sex poses the harmful effect of engendering an understanding of sexuality and personhood that is fluid; and

WHEREAS, Some public schools are encouraging parents and teachers to affirm the feelings of children whose self-perception of their own gender is at variance with their biological sex; and

WHEREAS, Some public schools are allowing access to restrooms and locker rooms according to children's self-perception of gender and not according to their biological sex; and

WHEREAS, The state of New Jersey prohibits licensed counselors from any attempt to change a child's "gender expression"; and

WHEREAS, These cultural currents run counter to the biblical teaching as summarized in *The Baptist Faith and Message*, Article III, that "Man is the special creation of God, made in His own image. He created them male and female as the crowning work of His creation. The gift of gender is thus part of the goodness of God's creation"; now, therefore, be it

RESOLVED, That the messengers to the Southern Baptist Convention meeting in Baltimore, Maryland, June 10–11, 2014, affirm God's good design that gender identity is determined by biological sex and not by one's self-perception – a perception which is often influenced by fallen human nature in ways contrary to God's design (Ephesians 4:17-18); and be it further

RESOLVED, That we grieve the reality of human fallenness which can result in such biological manifestations as intersexuality or psychological manifestations as gender identity confusion and point all to the hope of the redemption of our bodies in Christ (Romans 8:23); and be it further

RESOLVED, That we extend love and compassion to those whose sexual self-understanding is shaped by a distressing conflict between their biological sex and their gender identity; and be it further

RESOLVED, That we invite all transgender persons to trust in Christ and to experience renewal in the Gospel (1 Timothy 1:15-16); and be it further

RESOLVED, That we love our transgender neighbors, seek their good always, welcome them to our churches and, as they repent and believe in Christ, receive them into church membership (2 Corinthians 5:18-20; Galatians 5:14); and be it further

RESOLVED, That we regard our transgender neighbors as image-bearers of Almighty God and therefore condemn acts of abuse or bullying committed against them; and be it further

RESOLVED, That we oppose efforts to alter one's bodily identity (e.g., cross-sex hormone therapy, gender reassignment surgery) to refashion it to conform with one's perceived gender identity; and be it further

RESOLVED, That we continue to oppose steadfastly all efforts by any governing official or body to validate transgender identity as morally praiseworthy (Isaiah 5:20); and be it further

RESOLVED, That we oppose all cultural efforts to validate claims to transgender identity; and be it finally

RESOLVED, That our love for the Gospel and urgency for the Great Commission must include declaring the whole counsel of God, proclaiming what Scripture teaches about God's design for us as male and female persons created in His image and for His glory (Matthew 28:19-20; Acts 20:27; Romans 11:36).

6.3. Appendix 3: Joan or John? An Ethical Dilemma
Russell D. Moore

6.3.1. Southern Baptist Journal of Theology, 13.2 (2009): 52-56.

Russell D. Moore is Dean of the School of Theology and Senior Vice President for Academic Administration at The Southern Baptist Theological Seminary, where he also serves as Professor of Christian Theology and Ethics.

Dr. Moore is a Preaching Pastor at the Fegenbush campus of Highview Baptist Church in Louisville, Kentucky, where he ministers weekly. He is a senior editor of Touchstone: A Journal of Mere Christianity and is the author of Adopted for Life: The Priority of Adoption for Christian Families and Churches (Crossway, 2009).

Editor's Note: As explained below, the following is a five-part response by Dr. Moore to an ethical question posed to his Southern Seminary ethics class. We have included it in this issue of SBJT as a wonderful example of theology in practice, especially in relation to the doctrine of human beings. Systematic theology is not merely the affirmation of particular truths that Scripture teaches, even though it is that. It is also the application of those truths to all of life with the goal of helping the church live out the Gospel in our daily lives to the glory of God. One can learn a lot about a person's theology when one sees how it is applied to real life situations and what is given below is a fine example of seeking to take the whole counsel of God and to apply it to real ethical issues that we face. Regardless of whether you would have answered the question precisely in the way Dr. Moore answers it, may this article spur us on to work hard at bringing all of our thought and lives captive to Christ and to his Word.

Every year at the conclusion of my Survey of Christian Ethics class at Southern Seminary, I give my students a final ethical situation to answer for their final examination. They are graded not on their conclusion, but on how they arrived there. They answer, and then we discuss it communally as a class. The question below is this year's dilemma. Also included is my five-part response to the question originally published at www.russellmoore.com in May 2009.

The Question

This question takes place sometime in the future, in your ministry. Joan is a fifty-year-old woman who has been visiting your church for a little over a year. She sits on the third row from the back, and usually exits during the closing hymn, often with tears in her eyes. Joan approaches you after the service on Sunday to tell you that she wants to follow Jesus as her Lord. You ask Joan a series of diagnostic questions about her faith, and it is clear she understands the gospel. She still seems distressed though. When you ask if she's repented of her sin, she starts to cry and grit her teeth.

"I don't know," she says. "I don't know how ... I don't know where to start ... Can I meet with you privately?" You, Joan, and a godly Titus-2-type women's ministry leader in your church meet in your office right away, and Joan tells you her story. She wasn't born Joan. She was born John. From early on in John's life, though, he felt as though he was "a woman trapped in a man's body." Joan says, "I don't mean to repeat that old shopworn cliché, but it really is what I felt like." Joan tells you that when she was twenty she began the process of "transitioning" from life as a man to life as a woman. She underwent extensive hormone therapy, followed by extensive plastic surgery – including so-called "gender reassignment surgery." She has lived for the past thirty years – physically and socially – as a woman. "I want to do whatever it takes to follow Jesus," Joan tells you. "I want to repent ... I just, I don't know how to do it. I am surgically now a woman. I've taken hormones that give me the appearance and physical makeup of a woman," she says. "Even if I were to put on a suit and tie right now, I'd just look like a woman with a suit and tie. Not to mention the fact that, well, I am physically ... a woman. To complicate matters further," Joan says through tears, "I adopted my daughter, Clarissa, when she was eight months old, and she's ten years old now. She doesn't know about my past life as ... as a man. She just knows me as her Mom. I know the sex change surgery was wrong. I know that my life is twisted. I'm willing to do whatever Jesus would have me to do to make it right," she says. "But what would Jesus have me to do?" Joan asks you, "Am I too messed up to repent and be saved? If not, what does it mean for me to repent and live my life as a follower of Jesus? What is right for me to do?"

Show me, step-by-step, what you would say to Joan. Show me what you would tell her to do, short-term and long-term, and show me why in terms of a Christian ethic. Use Scripture, Christian theology, and wisdom to demonstrate not just your final decisions, but how you arrived at them. You may use any resource that would be available to you in a real life pastoral situation. This includes Holy Scripture, books, articles, and the seeking of outside counsel from others. Furthermore, show me how you would lead the rest of your congregation to think through and act in this situation with the mind of Christ.

6.3.2. Did Jesus Die for Joan?

Put a bit more succinctly, Joan was born John, but has lived as Joan for thirty years. She has a daughter. She now is convicted of sin and wants to follow Christ. She'll do whatever Jesus would have her to do, but she needs some direction from you, her pastor. Now, let me begin by saying that I'm using the name "Joan" and the female pronouns here simply as a literary device, to postpone the debate a bit as to whether this person is really male or female. In class, I let my students bat around and debate one another about how this situation should best be handled, and then I weighed in. Here's what I think is at stake in this situation, and how a Christian ought to look at it. The first issue is the gospel. Christ Jesus came to save sinners. The Lord Jesus offered up his life as a sacrifice for this person (this isn't an extent of the atonement debate, so save that one for later), and his bloody cross and empty tomb are enough to reconcile any sinner, including this one, to God. The pastor should abandon any sense of revulsion because Joan's situation is "weird" or "perverted." All sin is weird and perverted. The fact that any of it (especially our own) seems "normal" to us is part of what we need the gospel for. The second issue is repentance. Repentance is necessary for salvation, as is articulated in the gospel message throughout the Scripture (Mark 1:15; Acts 3:19; 17:30). I think the account of our Lord's interaction with the rich young ruler (Luke 18:18-29) is in order here, as well as his confrontation by the Syro-Phoenocian woman (Mark 7:24-30). In both cases, Jesus probed in order to bring forth, in the first case, a visible lack of repentance, or, in the second, a visible manifestation of faith. The message Joan has heard is the same message every Christian has heard, "Come, follow me." The pastor wishes to know, as he would with any sinner, whether she's counted the cost of doing so. At the same time, the pastor ought to know there is no simple solution here. Whatever Joan does will leave havoc in its wake. Her daughter will either grow up with a "mother" who has deceived her all life long about the most basic aspect of who she is, and what their relationship is, or she will go through the trauma of discovering her Mom is actually her Dad.

My counsel would be, after discerning that Joan is truly trusting in Christ (and it certainly appears that she is), to make sure she understands that part of the sin she's walking away from is a root-level rebellion against the Creator. God's creation is good, and he does not create generic persons but "male and female," in his own image (Gen 1:27). In seeking to "become" a woman, John has established himself as a god, determining the very structure of his createdness. Part of the freedom that comes in Christ is his recognition that he is a creature, not a god, not a machine, not a freak. This means that the pastor should, in his role as an under-shepherd of Christ, start speaking to Joan as "John," and identifying him as "him." This will seem strange and discordant to Joan. Of course it will. What is going on in this person's life, however, is what goes on in every Christian's life. We've put on a "new man," crucifying the old way (Eph 4:21-24). We are a "new creation" with the past done away with (2 Cor 5:17). We have a "new name" (Rev 2:17) that seems strange and mystifying, with an extended family we have to learn to love and walk with. Joan is not going to "feel" like John, and that's okay. But the pastor must start ministering to him by helping him identify what peace looks like, what the destination is to which he's headed. And that's as a man. Furthermore, the pastor cannot deceive his congregation. He doesn't need to elaborate on every aspect of this person's past (any more than he would with any other repentant sinner). But the church baptizes, not an individual, and the church must know the person being baptized. To baptize one created a man as "my sister in Christ" (whatever the baptismal formula used) isn't doing justice to a God who speaks the truth. But that's only the start of the ethical and pastoral dilemmas erupting here.

6.3.3. Should the surgery be reversed?

To respond to the question as to whether "Joan" should go reverse her so-called "gender reassignment" surgery, my answer is no. First of all, no surgery can reassign gender. The surgery mangled John, and sought to create an illusion of a biological reality that isn't there. There is no way that this surgery can be "reversed," only another cosmetic illusion created on top of the old one. Additional surgery would only compound the problem. He should see himself as the equivalent of a biblical eunuch, someone wounded physically by his past sin, but awaiting wholeness in the resurrection from the dead. He should, though, stop taking the female hormones, allowing his body to revert to its (relatively) natural state. The issue for John is honesty, it seems to me. This means that he should present himself as what he is, a man created by God as such. This means he should identify himself as a man, and should start dressing in male clothing. This is going to be very, very difficult for him, and he will need his pastors and congregation to bear with him through all the stumbles and backsteps that will come along with this. The most difficult aspect of this new honesty, however, is not what restroom John uses or the name on his driver's license. It is how he presents himself to a young daughter who has only known him as "Mom."

6.3.4. What about the daughter?

The issue of how to deal with Clarissa is, admittedly, the most difficult part of this puzzle. A friend said including the daughter in the narrative was the "evil genius" part of the whole thing. For my students at Southern Seminary, the daughter was the most heart-wrenching part of the whole question, and those who had difficulty typically had difficulty at this point. I'm glad that such is the case. The compassion for this daughter, having her entire spectrum of reality turned over, is a mark of a Christian, and certainly a necessary trait for a sheep-herder of God's flock. First, let me say that I'm aware that "Joan" becoming "John" will wreak havoc on her daughter's life and psyche. I think such havoc will be unleashed either way, and that honesty at this point is less destructive than continuing the illusion. The question, at this point, is not whether the daughter will have a normal life or a traumatic one. The question is whether the people of Christ will be with her through the trauma. I would counsel Joan to tell her daughter at an appropriate (but not unduly delayed) time. This will be difficult, and John will need his pastor there, along with many godly women from the congregation who are willing to spend hours with this young girl. John should tell her that years before she was born, he was confused, and felt like he was a girl instead of a boy, and that he had spent the last thirty years trying to be a girl. He should tell his daughter, though, that something had changed, he was born again in Christ Jesus, and that means that he gets a new start. He should tell her that he loves her just the same, and that he'll always be here, but he wants her to know that Jesus is putting his life back together, as a man. This will be confusing and disruptive, but, with the wise counsel of his congregation and its pastors, John can visibly demonstrate before his daughter what life in Christ actually looks like: slow, painful, but, in the end, worth it for the sake of the gospel.

6.3.5. How should the church respond?

So, if John follows through at this point, what's the expectation of the church, and the responsibility of the congregation, for change in the life of a man who once thought himself a woman? In saying that I don't think Joan can continue to live as a "woman," I am not saying that regeneration will mean that he suddenly "feels" like a man. John is telling you the truth when he says that he has felt all of his growing-up life like a woman trapped in a man's body. He will probably not suddenly turn into a lumberjack. He will probably grapple with this issue for the rest of his life. I was saved from, among many other things, covetousness. Coveting seems natural to me. Not coveting is unnatural to me. There's not a day that goes by in which coveting isn't the easier, more natural thing for me. But I fight against covetousness because God is conforming me into the image of Christ (Rom 8:29; 2 Cor 3:18). He does this through suffering, through discipline, and through the warlike struggle of the Spirit against the flesh, the new creation against the satanic powers (Rom 5:3-5; Heb 12:5-11; 2 Cor 2:11). Your testimony is the same, if you're in Christ, with any number of sinful patterns and weak points in your life. The same will be true for John. Don't give up on him if he has setbacks, and don't give up on him if he still "feels" like a woman for the rest of his life. Keep pointing him to the gospel, and to the faith that hears and acts. John's presence in your congregation will probably mean that some Pharisaism will emerge. Some people will find John "freakish." Some of the men will be revolted by the whole idea, and will think they are asserting their masculinity by mocking or marginalizing him (even if just in subtle, eye-rolling sorts of ways). The responsibility of the pastor is to lead his people away from this destructiveness. John's life in the congregation can be a visible signal of the mercies of God. This means the church should, immediately upon receiving John as a repentant sinner, announce that his sin (not in part but the whole!) is nailed to the cross of Christ, buried with Jesus, and obliterated by his resurrection power. This means any ongoing gossip or judgment of John's sin or John's past is itself violence against the gospel, as well as divisiveness in the congregation, and will be disciplined as such. The shepherds must lead your people to receive John, as they were received by Christ (Rom 15:57). The pastors and leaders of the church can help people to see how they can help bear their brother's burdens (Gal 6:2). This means, first of all, that women in the congregation will be needed to help show his daughter what it means to be a godly woman. Some of them will want to take her into their homes and lives, being mothers and grandmothers in Christ for her (Titus 2:3-5). This also means that the men in the congregation should make a concerted effort to disciple John, receiving him into their circle of friendship, and showing him what it means to follow Christ, and what it means to be a man. For some of them, it will be awkward. So what? It seems awkward for the Lord Jesus to spend time with drunkards, prostitutes, and Gentiles like us, but he did it, and does it even now.

6.3.6. Why does it matter?

Since I posted the question about John/Joan, I've had two kinds of responses. Some Christians have said things along the lines of, "I'm glad I'm not in your ethics class! That question is hard!" Others though have said, "You know, that very situation happened in my church." We're going to have more and more so-called "transgendered" persons in American society, as the culture around us changes. A woman in my congregation told me the other day she was asked when giving blood, "What gender were you at birth?" Now, we could always bemoan this, and talk about how American culture is slouching toward Gomorrah. We should hope, if there are transgendered persons in the cities and towns and villages around us, that we will see them in our church pews. And we should pray, feverishly, that they will hear the gospel we're preaching as good news for them. This doesn't mean that we create a new "transgendered" Sunday school class. That's not good news at all; any more than a "coveters" Sunday school class would be good for me! A gospel church, though, is a church that says whatever you're running from or running to, Jesus offers you life. As long as you're alive, it is not too late for you to find new life in Christ. Jesus loves sinners, and we do too. You see, the scenario about "Joan" isn't really all that hypothetical. Chances are in your town right now, there are people in that situation. Why don't they show up in our churches? Is it because they doubt if our gospel is really addressed to them? Is it because we doubt it too? If Joan comes to your church this Sunday and hears the gospel, if "she" decides to throw away everything "she" knows and follow Christ, will your church be there to love him, and to show him how to stop pretending and to fight his way toward what he was created to be? Maybe it would take a Joan at the altar call to make us question whether we really believe what we say and what we sing. Is there really power, wonder-working power, in the blood of the Lamb? Is our gospel really good news for prodigal sons, even for sons so lost they once thought they were daughters?

6.4.   For further reading

6.4.1.   From a Conservative perspective

The Evangelical Alliance, *Transsexuality*, Carlisle: Paternoster Press, 2000.

Walt Heyer, *A Transgender's Faith*, Walt Heyer, 2015.

Paul McHugh, 'Transgenderism: A Pathogenic Meme,' *Public Discourse*, 10 June 2015, article at file:///C:/Users/Martin/Documents/EGGS%20PRT/Transgender/Transgenderism_%20A%20Pathogenic%20Meme%20_%20oPublic%20Discourse.html.

Lawrence S Meyer and Paul McHugh, 'Sexuality and Gender,' *The New Atlantis*, No. 50, Fall 2016 at http://www.thenewatlantis.com/publications/number-50-fall-2016.

Oliver O'Donovan, *Transsexualism, Issues and Argument*, Cambridge: Grove Book, 2007.

Vaughan Roberts, *Transgender*, The Good Book Company, 2016.

Mark Yarhouse, *Understanding Gender Dysphoria*, Downers Grove: IVP Academic, 2015.

6.4.2.   From a pro-transgender perspective

Christina Beardsley, *The Transsexual person is my neighbour*, 2007, at http://changingattitude.org.uk/resources/publications/the-transsexual-person-is-my-neighbour.

Christina Beardsley and Michelle O'Brien (eds.), *This is my body – Hearing the theology of transgender Christians*, London: Darton, Longman and Todd, 2016.

Megan K DeFranza, *Sex Difference in Christian Theology*, Grand Rapids: Eerdmans, 2015.

Marcella Althaus-Reid and Lisa Isherwood (eds.), *Trans/Formations*, London: SCM, 2009.

Justin Tanis , *Trans-Gendered, Theology, Ministry and Communities of Faith*, Cleveland: The Pilgrim Press, 2003.

Leanne McCall Tigert and Marren C. Tirabassi (eds.), *Transgendering Faith, Identity, Sexuality & Spirituality*, Cleveland: Pilgrim Press, 2004.

If you have enjoyed this book, you might like to consider

- *supporting the work of the Latimer Trust*
- *reading more of our publications*
- *recommending them to others*

See www.latimertrust.org for more information.

Latimer Books

GGC	*God, Gays and the Church: Human Sexuality and Experience in Christian Thinking*	eds. Lisa Nolland, Chris Sugden, Sarah Finch
WTL	*The Way, the Truth and the Life: Theological Resources for a Pilgrimage to a Global Anglican Future*	eds. Vinay Samuel, Chris Sugden, Sarah Finch
AEID	*Anglican Evangelical Identity – Yesterday and Today*	J.I.Packer, N.T.Wright
IB	*The Anglican Evangelical Doctrine of Infant Baptism*	John Stott, Alec Motyer
BF	*Being Faithful: The Shape of Historic Anglicanism Today*	Theological Resource Group of GAFCON
TPG	*The True Profession of the Gospel: Augustus Toplady and Reclaiming our Reformed Foundations*	Lee Gatiss
SG	*Shadow Gospel: Rowan Williams and the Anglican Communion Crisis*	Charles Raven
TTB	*Translating the Bible: From William Tyndale to King James*	Gerald Bray
PWS	*Pilgrims, Warriors, and Servants: Puritan Wisdom for Today's Church*	ed. Lee Gatiss
PPA	*Preachers, Pastors, and Ambassadors: Puritan Wisdom for Today's Church*	ed. Lee Gatiss
CWP	*The Church, Women Bishops and Provision: The Integrity of Orthodox Objections to the Proposed Legislation Allowing Women Bishops*	
TSF	*The Truth Shall Set You Free: Global Anglicans in the 21st Century*	ed. Charles Raven
LMM	*Launching Marsden's Mission: The Beginnings of the Church Missionary Society in New Zealand, viewed from New South Wales*	eds. Peter G Bolt, David B. Pettett

9 781906 327491